How to Solve Your
PEOPLE PROBLEMS

How to Solve Your PEOPLE PROBLEMS

JANE ALLAN

KOGAN
PAGE

First published in Great Britain in 1989 by
Kogan Page Limited, 120 Pentonville Road,
London N1 9JN

Reprinted 1989, 1990

British Library Cataloguing in Publication Data

Allan, Jane
  How to solve your people problems
  1. Personnel management
  I. Title
  658.3

  ISBN 1-85091-653-5
  ISBN 1-85091-654-3 Pbk

Printed and bound in Great Britain by
Biddles Ltd, Guildford and King's Lynn

Contents

Preface

This book has been written for anyone who has made management mistakes simply because there was no quick way to find a solution to a demanding problem. Often, answers are there, but they take time to find and sometimes you just don't have the time. This book is intended to make very easy reading and will take you to the solution to your problem as quickly as you'll let it.

There are two ways of using this book:

1. If you face any one of the following people problems, all you have to do is to turn to the relevant chapter and read. The chapters include examples of forms and checklists wherever possible to make the use of the information easier.

    *   Chapter 3, Recruitment
    *   Chapter 4, Avoiding Recruitment
    *   Chapter 5, Appraisal
    *   Chapter 6, Discipline
    *   Chapter 7, Supervision
    *   Chapter 8, Delegation
    *   Chapter 9, Motivation
    *   Chapter 10, Understanding People
    *   Chapter 11, Difficult People
    *   Chapter 12, Conflict
    *   Chapter 13, Negotiation
    *   Chapter 14, Communication

2. If you know you have a problem, but don't know how best to categorise it, you will want to turn to the decision charts in Chapter 2 before reading any further. Chapter 2 is made up of the kind of questions, rhetorical or open, that you may ask from time to time during your business life; questions that need answers, which take time to find. Chapter 2 tries to direct your mind to some of the solutions that lie within the other chapters of the book. Not all of the chapters suggested will be the obvious place to look, but they may well offer the right solution, however surprising.

How to Solve Your People Problems

Finally, Chapter 1 should be reread from time to time. This chapter tries to set the nature of people's behaviour into context. It is a short chapter, but you need to think about it and apply it to the people you are trying to manage, the problems you are trying to solve and not least to yourself. It is hoped that you will come out of this book with a better understanding of yourself, which will, of course, help you to solve all your other people problems too.

Jane Allan

Chapter 1
Introduction

What are people problems?

It would all be so much easier if it weren't for people. Customers, clients, colleagues, bosses, subordinates, they all react and behave; and it's their behaviour that makes working life so difficult.

A problem is simply the difference between expectations and results. The term 'people problems' covers a variety of situations; this book is intended to cover the most common of them. Reading has been deliberately cut to the minimum; checklists and forms give quickly absorbed ideas to get you out of the problem situation you find yourself in. But before looking at these problem situations, consider whether your behaviour patterns may be part of the cause of the problems you face.

Behaviour

At the root of people problems is the behaviour of both parties concerned.

Behaviour breeds behaviour
It is really a case of 'do as you would be done by'. if you are angry and you let that anger show, anyone you deal with will become angry too. If, on the other hand, you quash your anger and behave in a friendly and helpful manner, the other party will be friendly and helpful too.

Taking this line of thinking further, questions lead to answers, and acknowledgement of the speaker leads to an even longer and more detailed answer. Cutting someone short leads to silence and no information at all whereas disagreeing generally leads to interruptions.

You can choose your own behaviour
While it is tempting to follow the behaviour pattern suggested by another party to any conversation, you still have the choice of

remaining your own person. Responding to anger with anger only leads to an argument; responding instead with a calm, helpful manner will take away the anger and lead to a solution to the problem.

You can use your behaviour to hinder or help each meeting

This type of behaviour is very easy to put into effect: you could decide to ignore people to prove your superiority and hinder any discussion; on the other hand, you could decide to be friendly and helpful, thereby ensuring that the outcome is a success. You can smile at people to make them feel welcome, or frown to make them feel a nuisance. You can take everything personally to make sure they clam up, or relax and let meetings proceed smoothly.

To be convincing, visual and verbal behaviour must tell the same story

Your body language must match your words. When you say something positive, a smile reinforces the message, a frown confuses. Avoiding eye contact makes people suspicious; looking them in the face shows openness and interest.

Body language checklist

How to appear defensive

Avoid eye contact, looking away as soon as it occurs. Cross your arms and keep your hands clenched. Keep rubbing your nose or one eye or one ear. Lean as far away as possible from the other person; cross your legs if seated and swivel your feet towards the door if standing.

These tactics should get the other people on the defensive too and ensure failed communication.

How to appear anxious

Blink frequently and lick your lips. Try clearing your throat regularly too. Tug at one ear and put a hand over your mouth when speaking to make all conversation indistinct. Open and close your hands frequently. If you are sitting down, keep fidgeting in your chair and jig your legs up and down.

Such behaviour should ensure a total atmosphere of nervous tension, which is bound to stifle any real communication.

How to appear aggressive

Stare at the other person, preferably over the top of any spectacles. If you don't wear spectacles, try raising your eyebrows in exaggerated disbelief or amazement; or you could always wear an 'I've heard it all before' smile. Point your finger at the other person or thump the table. If that fails, grab the back of your neck and rub it while frowning. Stand while the other person remains seated and then stride around so they have to keep moving to keep you in sight. If you decide to sit, lean back in your chair, legs splayed and hands clasped behind your head.

This approach should terrify even the strongest of individuals and ensure total communication failure.

Of course, if you would rather encourage communication and solve people problems, try the following three patterns of behaviour:

How to seem friendly and co-operative

Look the other person in the face without staring. Smile when you see them and nod your head as they talk. Keep your hands open, occasionally moving one hand to your face. Do not cross your arms. If you are sitting, keep your legs uncrossed and lean forward to show interest. If you are standing, move closer to the other person, but not so close as to be threatening. Remember that in the northern European countries, there is quite a large space-circle requirement with colleagues and strangers.

This behaviour will ensure a relaxed and friendly response from your colleagues and give every chance for successful communication.

How to seem confident

Look into the other person's eyes, thrusting your chin forward and avoiding blinking. Stand straight and at ease with your hands behind your back, or steeple your fingers; but at all times keep them away from your face. When you are seated, lean back with legs stretched out in front of you; at all times avoid sudden movements.

These tactics should ensure that the other party is aware of your strength of resolve and confidence in the outcome of any negotiation.

How to seem thoughtful

When listening, tilt your head to one side and make small agreement noises without interrupting the flow. Stroke your chin, or pinch the bridge of your nose. Take off any spectacles and put the ear piece into your mouth; remember this will hinder vision so try not to screw up your eyes to see. Lean forward to speak and back to listen keeping your legs still.

This approach should ensure that you seem thoughtful and willing to listen to the other person's point of view.

Positive versus negative behaviour

In every situation, there will be moments when your behaviour can rescue or destroy a chance at communication. Try to take the positive behaviour path at all times. On the following pages are pairs of statements describing the positive and negative responses to differing situations.

Negative behaviour	Positive behaviour
1. Lean away with hands clenched, arms crossed and legs crossed.	Lean forwards with hands open, arms uncrossed and legs uncrossed.
2. Look at the other person for less than 50 per cent of the time.	Look at the other person for approximately 60 per cent of the time.
3. Listen silently with no continuity noises and/or interruptions before the other person has had their say.	When listening nod and make listening noises such as 'um', 'yes', 'really'.
4. Wear a blank expression.	Smile.
5. Sit opposite the other person across a desk.	Sit beside the other person or at a 90-degree angle to them.

Negative behaviour	*Positive behaviour*
6. Don't use the other person's name or use it artificially so that it jars.	Use the other person's name early on in the conversation and smile when you use it.
7. Don't ask questions or ask closed questions.	Ask open questions.
8. Offer no summaries and don't check your understanding.	Summarise to the other person what you think they have said.
9. Stick rigidly to saying things that are routine and standard.	Say things that refer back to what the other person has said.
10. Don't acknowledge the other person's expressed feelings or point of view.	Show sympathy by saying you understand how the other person feels and can see things from their point of view.
11. Never explicitly agree with the other person.	When in agreement with the other person, openly say so and why.
12. Pick holes in the other person's ideas.	Build on the other person's ideas.
13. Criticise the other person.	Be non-judgemental towards the other person.
14. Disagree first, then say why.	If you have to disagree with the other person, give the reason first and then say that you disagree.
15. Be defensive and never admit to any inadequacy.	Admit it when you don't know the answer or when you have made a mistake.

Negative behaviour	*Positive behaviour*
16. Be secretive and withhold information from the other person, even though it affects them.	Openly explain what you are doing, or intend to do for the other person.
17. Be inconsistent with your body language.	Make sure your body language emphasises your speech.
18. Remain aloof, stand back and don't touch the other person.	Whenever possible, touch the other person, remembering the need for personal space.
19. Don't give the other person anything.	Give the other person something, even if it is only a name card or a piece of paper with notes on it.

Positive behaviour

The advantages of positive behaviour are not restricted to your own. Taking a positive attitude helps to encourage people to undertake tasks with more enthusiasm and to feel a sense of belonging to the organisation.

Belonging to a team

To make people feel part of the organisation, you have to emphasise a sense of belonging to the team. The answer is to make them feel, at all times, like a team by treating them as one. Ask for team views and listen to what they say. Very often the people at the sharp end of the operation have far better ideas for solving the organisation's problems than those in command.

If you treat people as a team, they will begin to think like a team, instead of as a bunch of individuals who are only interested in their own jobs. Once you have them thinking like a team, it's a short step to get them to act as a team.

Being a worthwhile member of a team

The art of making people feel positive about their jobs and their roles within the organisation is to give them confidence in their own abilities. After all, you recruited them in the first place, so they must have some perceived value to the team; now take the chance to enhance that value in their own eyes.

Set people a challenge from time to time, having first given them training or made sure they understand the challenge they are being offered. The most unlikely people will take up the challenge and succeed where you might have thought they would fail. Once they have succeeded, go out of your way to acknowledge the success, even if it is only the success of effort and the outcome was not as expected. A few words of thanks go a long way.

Try to be aware of the problems and personal difficulties that your staff encounter. You cannot solve their problems, but you can be fair in helping them to solve them by themselves. Never be afraid to show concern; remember how sympathy can often help during a trying time.

Doing a worthwhile job
Let people see that you think highly of their job and they will do so too. No one will understand all aspects of their job without explaining; give them the chance to understand by putting tasks into context and explaining the full effect of everything they do. When they have done the task, give them feedback, even if you feel the ultimate end is not their concern. People like to know the outcome of their actions and they like to be involved. After all, a large part of life is spent at work; if there is no interest there, life itself becomes rather dull.

Finally, always be aware that as an employer or leader you are a role model. The example you set is the one that people will follow; always make sure it is a good example. Don't knock the organisation to others, be loyal upwards to your bosses and downwards to your staff.

Now read on to solve the people problems that arise in any organisation.

Chapter 2
Now What?

Decision chart 1

Nobody seems to know what they are doing around here.

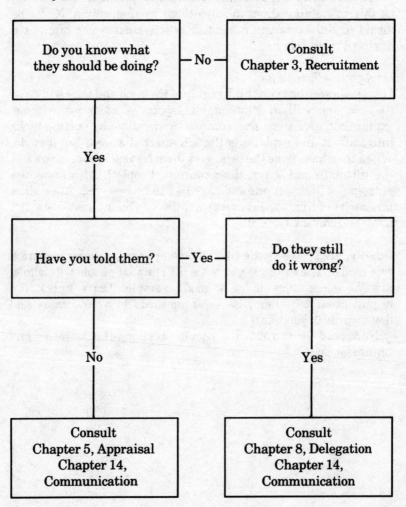

Decision chart 2

Nobody tells you anything.

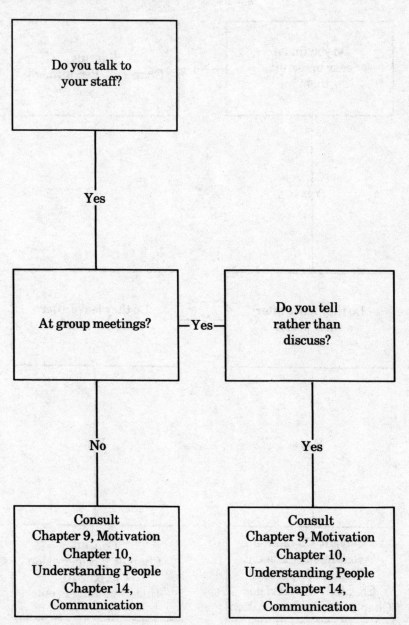

Decision chart 3

You can't seem to keep staff.

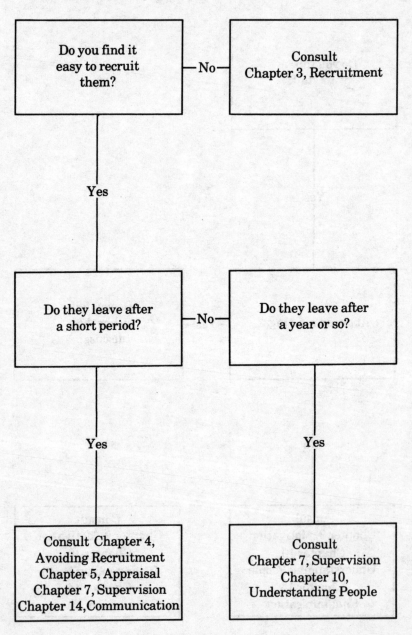

Decision chart 4

You can't seem to get staff at all.

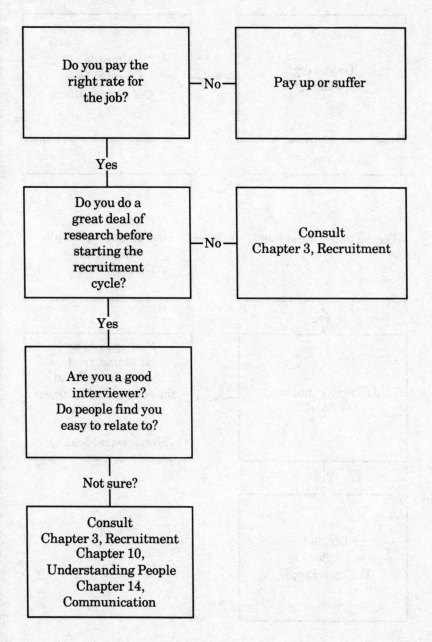

Decision chart 5

You can't seem to get through to them.

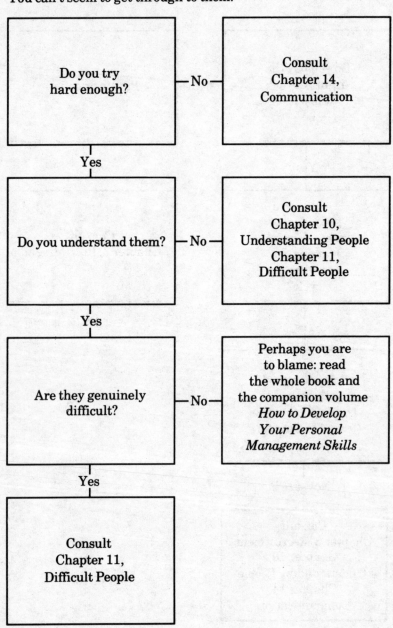

Do you try
hard enough?

— No —

Consult
Chapter 14,
Communication

Yes

Do you understand them?

— No —

Consult
Chapter 10,
Understanding People
Chapter 11,
Difficult People

Yes

Are they genuinely
difficult?

— No —

Perhaps you are
to blame: read
the whole book and
the companion volume
*How to Develop
Your Personal
Management Skills*

Yes

Consult
Chapter 11,
Difficult People

Decision chart 6

Standards seem to be slipping.

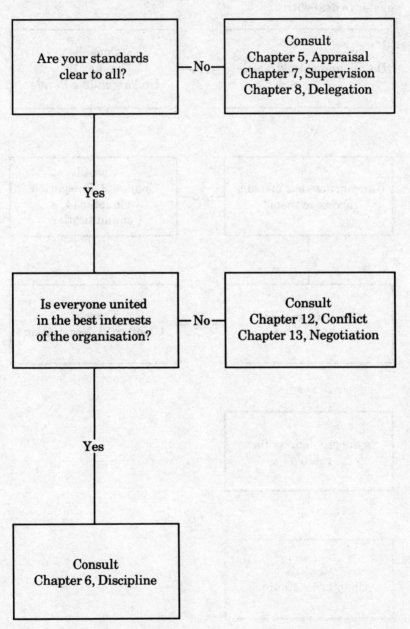

Are your standards clear to all? —No— Consult
Chapter 5, Appraisal
Chapter 7, Supervision
Chapter 8, Delegation

Yes

Is everyone united in the best interests of the organisation? —No— Consult
Chapter 12, Conflict
Chapter 13, Negotiation

Yes

Consult
Chapter 6, Discipline

How to Solve Your People Problems
Decision chart 7

You wish you didn't have to rely on people. Machines are so much easier to deal with.

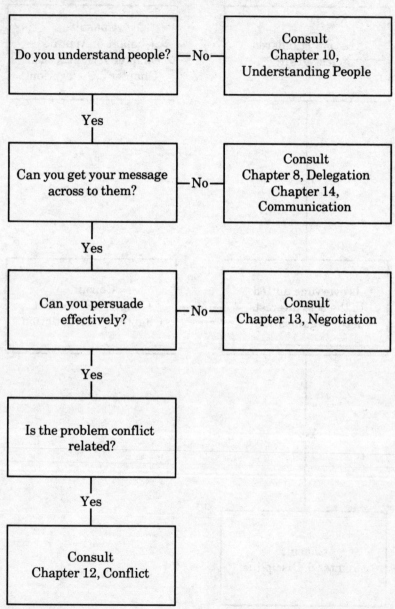

Do you understand people? —No— Consult Chapter 10, Understanding People

Yes

Can you get your message across to them? —No— Consult Chapter 8, Delegation Chapter 14, Communication

Yes

Can you persuade effectively? —No— Consult Chapter 13, Negotiation

Yes

Is the problem conflict related?

Yes

Consult Chapter 12, Conflict

Decision chart 8

X was the best member of the team. Now he has handed in his notice - what are you going to do?

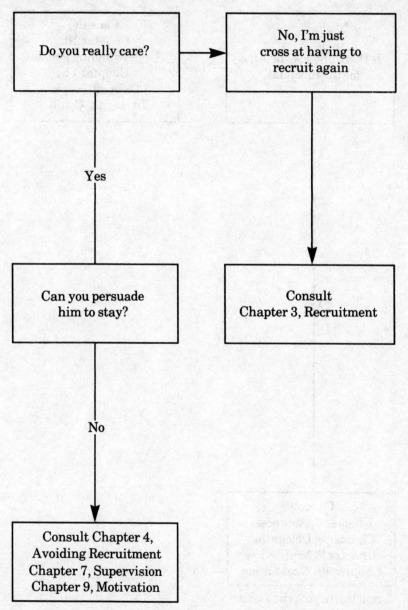

Decision chart 9

Just when things seem to be running smoothly, someone throws a tantrum and everything goes wrong.

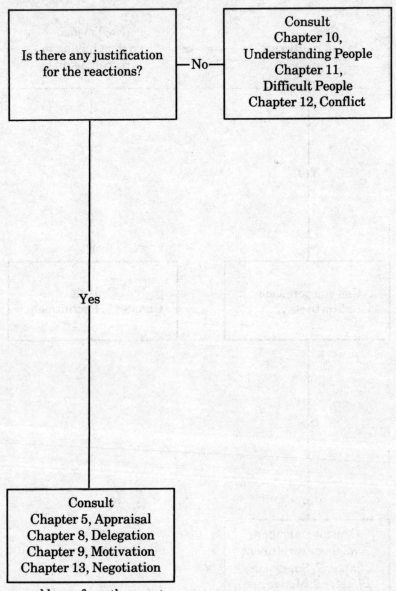

Is there any justification for the reactions? —No—

Consult
Chapter 10,
Understanding People
Chapter 11,
Difficult People
Chapter 12, Conflict

Yes

Consult
Chapter 5, Appraisal
Chapter 8, Delegation
Chapter 9, Motivation
Chapter 13, Negotiation

and learn from the event

Decision chart 10

How do you get a team to settle down to work?

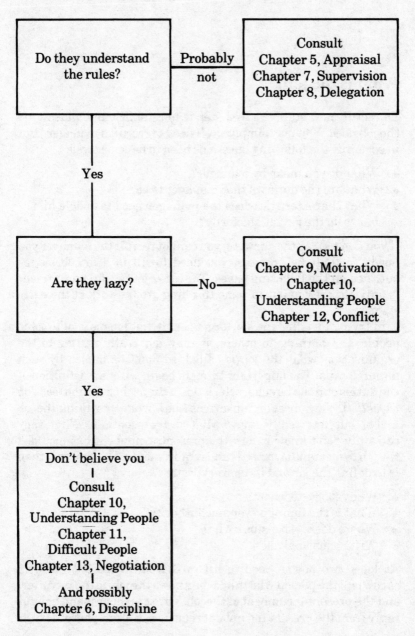

Chapter 3

Recruitment

What is the job?

To recruit new staff, the first step is to establish and understand the job need. You may simply say 'I need to recruit a manager.' But in so doing, the following questions need to be considered:

- What do you mean by manager?
- What are the duties of that manager to be?
- What characteristics does the manager need to enable him or her to do the job satisfactorily?

If you don't know the answers, you cannot recruit the manager you need. To find the answers, you need to fill in a few forms, as outlined on the following pages. The art of successful recruitment is only easy if you put in some thinking groundwork at the early stages.

In trying to define the job, forget the title; it means a lot to some people and nothing to others; it may not really matter to the organisation what the job is called, so don't be misled by such minor details. The important thing to begin with is a definition of the duties and the key characteristics of the job in question (see *Job checklist*). Now, most organisations know what they think the job to be, but few really know what it truly entails. What they certainly don't know is how the present incumbent has moulded the job to meet his own needs and requirements. The first step then is to define the job and its characteristics:

- Who reports to whom?
- What is the line of power and authority?
- Where does responsibility lie?
- Write a job analysis.

At least two people need to fill in this form (see *Job analysis checklist*): the person who thinks he knows the job, ie the recruiter, and the present incumbent of the job. To get an honest and helpful reply from the present incumbent requires an atmosphere of trust.

Job checklist

Job title
This may have to be changed later when you consider how to sell
the job.

Job structure
Fill in here a diagrammatic picture of the job and its position in the
hierarchical structure of the organisation.

Reporting to
What happens now?

Responsible for
Real not token responsibility.

Authority
Real, including the usurped variety.

Power
Real, including the usurped variety.

Responsible to
In a direct line? Via someone else? Ultimate responsibility needs
to be noted here.

How to Solve Your People Problems

Duties
What is done, not what you'd like to be done.

_____
_____
_____
_____
_____
_____
_____
_____
_____
_____
_____
_____
_____
_____
_____
_____
_____
_____
_____
_____
_____
_____
_____
_____
_____
_____
_____
_____
_____
_____
_____
_____
_____

Job analysis checklist
A time audit to be filled in by the present incumbent.

Job title

_____

Duties carried out generally

_____
_____
_____
_____
_____
_____
_____
_____

Duties carried out on
Two or three typical days should be selected so that a clear picture of the job can emerge.

9.00 am _____
10.00 am_____
11.00 am_____
12.00 am_____
13.00 hrs _____
14.00 hrs _____
15.00 hrs _____
16.00 hrs _____
17.00 hrs _____
Overtime_____

No good will come of treating it as evidence to be taken down and used against him or her.

Fine, so now you know the duties. Of course, there may be a discrepancy between the duties you thought were attached to the job and those that the present incumbent believes to be part of the job. Learn the lesson. With a change of personnel comes the opportunity to change the job; but only do so if it will achieve your desired ends.

Employee characteristics

Once the job need is established, further problems arise:

- Who will be capable of filling it?
- Who would want to fill it?
- What sort of person would the job suit?

It is too easy to over or under recruit: 'We need someone to keep all the accounting records in order.' 'Fine, let's recruit an accountant.' 'Well they cost money, big money, and when they get bored they cost even more money to replace.' 'Who needs an accountant? We'll get some part-timer to knock these books together.' Mistakes cost money too; sometimes even more than the savings could ever have been. The right person in the right job needs some careful thought.

Step 1: Establish realistic employee characteristics
Who has successfully held the post or a similar post before? Why were they seen as good at the job? To find your answer, you need to analyse their abilities, background, education and personal characteristics. First, pick one or two people who have held the post previously and of whom you thought highly. Then, fill in the *Employee characteristics checklist*. Now get someone else to complete the same exercise. Once all the forms are completed, it will be necessary to establish the degree of tolerable variance.

Step 2: What are the ideal characteristics of the future employee?
What are the ideal characteristics of the future employee? What are the specific requirements of the job? To find your answer you need to consider the job in great detail. What matters and what is just nice? The *Job analysis worksheet* now needs to be filled in.

Employee characteristics checklist

Name

Dates when post held

Title of position

Age

Education

A levels

Degree

Professional qualification

Personal details

Hobbies

Languages spoken

Other experience

Personality details
Cross out the words that do not apply.

shy: outward looking: people-person: thinker: authoritative: self-effacing: perfectionist: ideas-person: quick worker: thorough worker: craftsperson: creative: patient: impatient: broad-brush approach: systematic: drive: methodical: optimistic: cautious: homely.

Job analysis worksheet

Job
Working title only - remember you may have to change it later.

Directions
The statements in this worksheet describe skills and abilities required for various jobs. Please read each of the statements carefully. Indicate your opinion about their relative importance in the performance of the job by marking each statement either:

1. (very important)
2. (somewhat important)
3. (not very important)
4. (not important at all)

Answer every statement and take as much time as is needed to give each careful consideration.

- ☐ 1. Maintaining patience with difficult people and events.
- ☐ 2. Thinking of new and better ways of doing things and implementing them.
- ☐ 3. Selling a service or product.
- ☐ 4. Noticing likenesses or differences when comparing lists of names, numbers or other items.
- ☐ 5. Doing work under specific instructions or guidelines.
- ☐ 6. Working co-operatively under close supervision.
- ☐ 7. Working directly with others in order to get a job done.
- ☐ 8. Stimulating enthusiasm in order to get co-operation and results.
- ☐ 9. Handling small objects neatly without fumbling or dropping them.
- ☐ 10. Filling in standard record forms, production records, orders etc.
- ☐ 11. Compiling lists, numbers or similar information on a regular routine basis.
- ☐ 12. Making decisions and assuming responsibility for them.
- ☐ 13. Taking charge of others and directing their work.
- ☐ 14. Formulating strategy or goals for a particular development or activity within the company.
- ☐ 15. Doing the same task repeatedly rather than doing a variety of tasks.
- ☐ 16. Following an established route.

☐ 17. Using independent initiative to solve unexpected problems.

☐ 18. Remaining lively and responsive when working with people for extensive periods of time.

☐ 19. Making decisions when no established policy exists for guidance.

☐ 20. Spending most of one's time with people rather than with machinery, processes or paperwork.

☐ 21. Remaining pleasant and friendly while dealing with people all day long.

☐ 22. Organising one's own work and using time effectively.

☐ 23. Staying at the same workstation for long periods.

☐ 24. Working carefully with numbers, making measurements or handling money.

☐ 25. Remembering details.

☐ 26. Influencing people to change their attitudes or opinions.

☐ 27. Remembering written or spoken instructions accurately enough to carry them out when working alone.

☐ 28. Meeting scheduled deadlines.

☐ 29. Building team work and co-operation between work groups.

☐ 30. Keeping up with what is going on in other parts of the company and with the problems and goals of the company as a whole.

☐ 31. Drawing neat and precise diagrams, charts or graphs.

☐ 32. Seeing how a situation looks to another person and understanding how he or she feels about it.

☐ 33. Responding to criticism or antagonism in a co-operative manner.

☐ 34. Being responsible for waste control or quality control.

☐ 35. Making sure others follow rules and procedures.

☐ 36. Checking detail work for errors.

With the help of these two forms you should now know who you need for the job. It may be possible to find an exact match, but the chances are that you will not find the perfect candidate. Establish the most and least important characteristics and draft your recruitment guide incorporating a tolerable degree of variance.

Remember that a blinkered view that looks only for the perfect soul, does not see possible and effective alternatives, so try to be as flexible as possible.

Recruitment guide

Now, you need to draft a working *Recruitment guide,* as illustrated by the following:

Recruitment guide

	Essential	Important	Nice but not vital
Education	☐	☐	☐
	☐	☐	☐
	☐	☐	☐
Qualification	☐	☐	☐
	☐	☐	☐
	☐	☐	☐
Personal background	☐	☐	☐
	☐	☐	☐
	☐	☐	☐
Personality	☐	☐	☐
	☐	☐	☐
	☐	☐	☐
Work-related experience	☐	☐	☐
	☐	☐	☐
	☐	☐	☐
Non-relevant experience	☐	☐	☐
	☐	☐	☐
	☐	☐	☐
Attitude	☐	☐	☐
	☐	☐	☐
	☐	☐	☐

The recruitment guide is only the working document for you to start the long haul to successful recruitment. Since you now know the type of person you need, you will have to go about attracting that individual and no others. How will your ideal candidate respond? Will he or she expect to use a recruitment agency; or will they look for the job in a newspaper advertisement? Which newspaper will your candidate read? What phrases and titles will attract them to the job? All the hard work to date will be in vain if the advertisement or agency briefing is wrong.

Briefing an agency is easy. Since you know certain precise guidelines, give them to the agency and make sure they stick to them. But perhaps you would prefer to tackle the recruitment through newspaper advertising and that's not quite so easy.

To draft your successful advertisement, you need to find the answers to the following questions:

- Who do you want to reply?
- What information will they need to enable them to make a decision to apply for the job?
- How will they be made aware of the vacancy?
- Why should they want to work for you?

'Who' is simple - you have the answer; but how can you attract the ideal who? You can start by eliminating all prejudices and personal hangups; who cares where the advertisement appears or what it looks like, as long as it does the trick? Probably the views of the present incumbent will help here. Where did they go to find a job? What sort of advertisement summoned their response?

The information needed is likely to be precise: salary and perks, location and duties will be essential to get the replies you seek. No salary and there is no measure for the prospective employee. No location and the worst fears may be justified; applying for your own job for example! No indication of the duties and the employee has no idea if he or she is capable of the job.

For your advertisement to work, it needs to be seen. Black is more visible than grey; use strong lines and borders. Logos give immediate identification; use them to make your identity clear. Top right-hand page spots cost more because they are seen more often and first; pay the surcharge, it is worth it.

Why you? Perhaps because you are just the type of organisation the prospective employee is looking for. Which means the advertisement must reveal something about the organisation seeking the new employee. But what kind of an organisation is it?

- caring, paternal employer;
- aggressive thrusting go-getters;
- international, big employer;
- life-time employers;
- unique in its market place;
- small personal, friendly organisation;
- tomorrow's market leaders;
- today's market leaders;
- yesterdays's market leaders;
- up-market, exclusive;
- down-market, cheap and cheerful;
- expensive but reliable;
- cheap but effective.

If the truth hurts, it is still better to live with that rather than an illusion. The truth about your organisation, in the style and language, in the words and illustrations, will attract people who really do want to work for you, not some improbable palace of your dreams.

What section of the buying public/readers/clients and customers typify the target recruitment audience?

- intellectual;
- creative;
- wealthy;
- wheeler-dealer:
- growth;
- long-established;
- lazy;
- go-getter;
- thinker;
- producer;
- small business;
- large business;
- specific business type.

Write the advertisement for the people you have realised you need.

What sales documents does the organisation have that will help you to sell well at interview and to write the successful advertisement in the first instance?

- brochure describing the organisation;
- in-house journal or newsletter;
- report and accounts;

- courses brochure;
- external-based selling material;
- marketing product, TV advertising, media advertising, poster;
- information leaflet;
- technical publication;
- application form;
- the interviewer.

All these items come from an exercise in communication on behalf of the employer. If your communication exercise is wrong, the recruitment will be wrong too.

Remember, a recruitment exercise is simply a negotiation between a person with something to sell and a person with a need to buy:

Seller	*Buyer*
Employee with talents and skills	Employer
Employer with interesting job	Employee

If you do not take steps to sell the organisation to the right buyer, you will be forced into the role of passive buyer with little or no control over the employee/seller's interests in your organisation.

Application form

Fine, you wrote the right advertisement, but what are you going to ask the applicants to do? Sell on their terms or yours? There is a school of thought that suggests that every candidate should submit his or her own curriculum vitae (CV); that way they will show most effectively their true characteristics. Individual CVs are fine, but they are not easy to compare, one with another. So now you need an application form. Back comes the recruitment guide; what do you need to know to enable you to make a fair and sensible interview decision. Consider the *Application form contents checklist*.

Application form contents checklist
The following are essential:

- name;
- addresses (if recruiting undergraduates, term time and other);
- age;
- date of birth;

- sex (some people spell their names very strangely!);
- marital status;
- nationality;
- education;
- qualifications;
- referees;
- previous employment details, including experience, job title and reasons for leaving.

Not essential, but very important if you are to make the right selection for interview, will be:

- information that gives clues to personality and character, eg hobbies and interests;
- an opportunity to describe experiences and non-relevant information, which may reveal peripheral skills, eg car driver, languages spoken;
- reason behind the application, giving the candidate an opportunity to explain why he is interested in a particular post.

Perhaps you also need to know:

- present salary;
- political views;
- religion.

Some recruiters feel they need:

- a photograph;
- to examine the candidate's handwriting;
- to know the candidate's ability to write figures;
- to find out the extent of technical and academic knowledge held by the candidate.

It may well be that you do not wish to interview every applicant who submits an application form to you. Your application form will need to enable you to make the right selection. The right selection must be:

- *Within the law:* Equal opportunities legislation requires you to consider men and women equally for the post. Nor can you discriminate on ethnic or religious grounds.
- *In your interests:* Make sure each form is considered carefully.
- *Consistent:* If necessary, develop a standard checklist to ensure that you do consider all applications consistently.

Write your own application form; a possible example is given below.

Application for employment
Address of the office to which the form is to be sent

We are concerned that, should we summon you to interview as a result of this application, the interviewer is able to make the best use of the short time available. For this reason, it will help us greatly if you will fill in all our questions and then add any further information you feel we should have concerning your application. Please attach a current photograph to your application form.

Please complete the form as legibly as possible, preferably using black or blue ink to enable us to make photocopies where necessary.

Name _____

Title (Mr/Mrs/Miss/Other) _____ *Sex* (M/F) _____

Home Address _____

_____ *Post code* _____

Address for correspondence (If different from above)

_____

_____ *Post code* _____

Job for which you are applying _____

Please answer the following questions about yourself.

Date of birth _____ *Age* _____

Marital status _____

Nationality _____ *State of health* _____

How to Solve Your People Problems

Please answer the following questions about your education. If any question does not apply to you, just score through the answer space.

Secondary education

School _____

GCE O-levels/GCSE passes _____

_____

_____

GCE A-levels _____

_____

Further education

University/college _____

Degree/qualification _____ *Level* _____

Vocational education

Professional body _____

Exam details (Please give exams passed and dates of passing)

_____

_____

_____

Qualification _____

Other (Please give details of qualification and method of attaining it)

_____

_____

_____

In this section of the application form we should like to learn more about you, your hobbies, capabilities and interests. Please use the space at the end to augment the questions we have asked with any information you feel is relevant.

Hobbies _____

_____

_____

Other interests _____

_____

_____

_____

Do you hold a current driving licence? _____

Do you own a car? _____

Do you speak any foreign languages? (Please indicate fluency)

_____

_____

Please use the space below to add any information you wish.

_____

_____

_____

_____

_____

On this section of the application form we wish to find out about your work experience to date. Please fill in the following section, giving details of your current employment first, followed by other employments in reverse date order.

Employer	*Job title*	*Joined*	*Left*

Reason for leaving _____

_____

Employer	*Job title*	*Joined*	*Left*

Reason for leaving _____

_____

How to Solve Your People Problems

Employer	Job title	Joined	Left
_____	_____	_____	_____
_____	_____	_____	_____

Reason for leaving _____

_____

Employer	Job title	Joined	Left
_____	_____	_____	_____
_____	_____	_____	_____

Reason for leaving _____

_____

Why have you decided to apply to . . . .?

It helps us to know why you feel we are the right employer for you, or why you have chosen the career we offer.

_____

_____

_____

_____

_____

_____

Referees

Please give the names and addresses of two referees we can contact. No references will be taken up until we feel that we wish to offer you a position with us. All such offers will be subject to satisfactory references. We also reserve the right to contact your present employer once an offer has been made and accepted by yourself.

Name _____ *Title* _____

Address _____

_____ *Post code* _____

Name _____ *Title* _____

Address _____

_____ *Post code* _____

Please use this final page to give us any further details that might help your application. In particular, we should like to know of any non-relevant or voluntary work which nevertheless has contributed to your personal development to date.

Relevant non-career employment

_____
_____
_____
_____
_____
_____

Voluntary work

_____
_____
_____
_____
_____
_____

Interviewing

Once the replies start to come in you are faced with a decision. Which candidates will you interview? Use your employment guide to match the key characteristics and produce your interviewee shortlist. Some candidates will be obvious, but not all. If in doubt, it is wiser to interview. Whatever you decide, you must act promptly. Telephone if possible to arrange an interview and confirm the date and time in writing.

Next, you need to plan the actual interview. It is your greatest opportunity to sell to your prospective employee; do not lose that opportunity. Make sure at all times of the following:

- The interview takes place at the stated time.
- The interviewer is ready to interview on time.
- The interviewer has read the submitted application form.
- The interviewer has both power and authority to make a decision.
- The interview room is ready and receptive.
- Reception are aware of the individuals due to attend.

If phone calls or visitors disturb your interview, you will cease to concentrate and the candidate will think you are either inefficient or else that you have no interest in him.

Make sure you remember the candidate's name and can refer to points he has written on the interview form. This really means that you need to allow time to study that form before the interview and not merely to rely on surreptitious glances during the interview itself.

Be well laid out; make sure you retain the advantage and that you can see your candidate clearly. The best layout places no barriers between the candidate and the interviewer. The best interview room is relaxing with conversation pieces in it. Any desk covered with paper is a distraction and a barrier to easy conversation. A separate discussion area with a small surface for papers makes for a more effective interview.

Hence, before you start to interview, be prepared - no impression is worse than the interviewer who has to search for papers, pens or his colleagues:

- cancel all phone calls or divert them;
- indicate that you are engaged;
- read the application form beforehand;
- think about the candidate;
- make notes;
- collect together all the relevant papers;
- alert any other people who need to be involved;
- make sure everything you need is to hand - pen, handkerchief, paper, telephone, checklist;
- make sure the interview area is ready - Is it tidy? Does it need to be? Are there two chairs? What layout has been chosen? Is it welcoming?
- demonstrate interest in the candidate.

Now plan your interview. After all, you will have only an hour or so to make a very expensive decision; you need to make the right one.

Interview Plan

1. *Introduction*
   Take time to introduce yourself. (2 minutes)
2. *Easing*
   Take time to discuss pleasantries. (2 minutes)
3. *Background*
   Check on any details relating to the candidate's background. (5 to 10 minutes)
4. *Interests/hobbies*
   Allow the candidate time to enlarge on the information presented on the form. (5 to 10 minutes)
5. *Qualification*
   Discuss in reasonable detail the candidate's approach to study and examinations. Assess any likely future results (trainees only). (5 to 10 minutes)
6. *Experience*
   Consider in depth the experience the candidate claims (tests?). (10 to 15 minutes)
7. *Previous employment*
   Invite the candidate to illustrate his reasons for employment changes and indicate the value and type of experience gained. (5 to 10 minutes)
8. *Other experience*
   Invite the candidate to draw to your attention any further details about his career or interests. (5 to 10 minutes)
9. *Information*
   Tell the candidate in more detail about the post for which he has applied. (10 to 15 minutes)
10. *Questions*
    Invite and reply to any questions. (5 to 10 minutes)
11. *Conclusion*
    Allow time to discuss any further points. Give both parties the opportunity to open subjects for discussion. (5 to 10 minutes)
12. *Farewells*
    Take time to say goodbye to the candidate pleasantly, indicating when you are likely to be in touch with the results of the interview. (2 minutes)

Total time for interview: 61/96 minutes

How to Solve Your People Problems

It is a very clever interviewer who can remember sufficient detail about everyone seen during the course of a day's interviewing. You need to take notes. Constant essay writing can distract from the main purpose of the interview: the need to get to know the candidate. Watching someone write down all that is said can be very unnerving and make any candidate nervous. To avoid these problems you need:

- to make the bulk of your notes after the inverview is over;
- to allow time for that;
- a system of quick grading which is very helpful;
- a standard system which will ensure consistency.

The *Fact checklist*, which is outlined on the following pages, can be used to fill in detail after the interview is over, or even to score a quick 1 to 6 without unduly distracting the candidate or the interviewer. Every fact checklist will be different because it will be based on the recruitment guide specific to each job.

This candidate was:

Outstanding _____

Above average _____

Acceptable _____

Doubtful _____

Reject _____

Fact checklist

Person specification	Indicating behaviour/ areas of questioning	Evidence obtained	Rating 1 2 3 4 5 6
Education (Specify your minimum requirements)	Evident from application form - clarifying questions only		
Obligatory working conditions Normal hours Overtime required Travelling distance Salary expectation Willingness to stay	Evident from application form - clarifying questions only		
Intellectual demands of the job, eg General ability	Performance in exams Level of achievement outside work Use of language, concepts Information in discussion		
Creative ability	New solutions to problems		
Judgemental ability	Major decisions taken and reasons Level of analysis of work Practicality of decisions taken		

How to Solve Your People Problems

Person specification	Indicating behaviour/ areas of questioning	Evidence obtained	Rating 1 2 3 4 5 6
Skill with people			
Physical appearance	Roles at school, college work, at home		
Ability to work alone/ in groups	Leisure activities		
Ability to communicate	Self-expression		
Ability to motivate	Problems encountered, how handled		
Ability to build new relationships	Social activities enjoyed		
Tact	Social activities avoided		
Adjustment			
Emotional maturity	Actions and comments showing self-knowledge, recognition of own strengths and weaknesses		
	Types and degrees of stress encountered		
	How was stress handled?		
Motivation			
Career hopes	Activities persistently pursued		
Persistent interest	Persistent plans and endeavours		
Interest in business	Obstacles and deficiencies overcome		
No extreme views or commitments	Comments and judgements on own performance		
Commitment to high standards	Future goals		
Drive			
Energy and persistence	Personal level of achievement		

Person specification	Indicating behaviour/ areas of questioning	Evidence obtained	Rating 1 2 3 4 5 6
Ambitions	Obstacles accepted/ overcome Length of time accepted for achieving goals Self-discipline in reaching goals		
General good health			

Once the interview is over all you have to do is make a decision. Which of the candidates will you offer the job to? It is not always easy. Sometimes you will know exactly the right candidate, but other times none will be perfect; many will have varying degrees of perfection. Which one will you employ? Only you can have all the knowledge to come to a conclusion; but consider the following:

- Is a deep-seated instinct saying 'yes' despite the facts that say 'no'?
- How realistic has your instinct been in the past?
- Have you consulted someone else?
- Have you tried psychological testing?
- Call the candidate back for another interview and involve at least one other person.
- Take the opinion of any member of staff to whom the candidate was introduced and who had an opportunity to spend time with him.
- Look carefully at the academic and past employment records of the candidate.
- Sleep on the decision, and allow your intuition to work.
- Toss a coin.

The interviewer endowed with instinct will often come to a conclusion that seems to stand without logical backing. Interviewing instinct is such that it may well be the correct conclusion, but the apparent reasoning will not be clear. Only experience can tell you how good or indifferent your instinct is likely to be. Don't entirely ignore it, however; let it help you to direct questions at the interview and let it contribute to your decision making.

How to Solve Your People Problems

Test your instinct by:

- analysing it immediately; writing down your vague reactions - eg wet hands, shuts eyes to speak, etc;
- use your reactions to examine existing staff;
- use psychological testing as a completely independent opinion.

Always keep the notes you have made regarding your instinctive reactions. Let them build up over a period of time; they will serve as a diary to help you gain knowledge of and confidence in your instinct.

If the decision really is too difficult to make alone, you might prefer to rely on independent testing. Psychological testing consists of two types: cognitive or intelligence testing, which is most useful in schools, and personality testing, which may be useful to all.

Personality testing is a scoring method of defining characteristics of the person tested. It cannot select right from wrong, act as God, measure maturity or intelligence, tell you anything about a person's social imprint or make your decisions for you. On the other hand, it can increase your knowledge of an interviewee's personality, let you find out what makes people tick, give an idea of their energy level, tell you things about a person it would not otherwise be easy to discover and give you better knowledge with which to make decisions.

Personality testing works by using some form of test, word or picture association and getting the individual being tested to react. Those reactions are then compared to a known and studied norm.

To be effective, personality tests must be valid; that is, they must be thoroughly tried and tested, straightforward but not transparently simple, and relevant and representative. They should have standard instructions, an easy system of marking and the facility to be used in any group size. No personality test will have right or wrong answers or a time limit.

If you decide to use such testing it will take time and patience to get people to accept tests as a good and useful thing. To prove your case, first test yourself, then test the bosses and finally test everyone else.

Chapter 4
Avoiding Recruitment

Recruitment is expensive, not merely in the cost of finding someone and paying the fees required by the agency, but in the expense of training the new individual and re-establishing the team. If you can avoid recruitment, you can save money and upset.

The checklist for avoiding recruitment is:

- Choose the right people in the first instance.
- Keep them once you've chosen them.
- Always consider the possibility of promotion before recruitment.
- Consider the opportunity of getting someone back.
- Think about changing the job to match the existing people.

Choosing the right people

Chapter 3 considered the art of successful recruiting. The major lesson to be learnt from that chapter is that anything that works well, takes time. The investment of the recruiter's time is the most essential one in ensuring that recruitment is a once-and-for-all exercise.

Keeping the right people

People stay in jobs for a number of reasons:

- The job satisfies their basic human needs (see Chapter 10).
- The job continues to motivate them (see Chapter 9).
- The job offers training and growth opportunities as yet not fully exploited (see Chapter 8).
- The job offers challenge and career development.
- The job offers a happy social environment with good team support.
- There is no better job to be found.
- They have reached their 'Peter Principle' (see page 53).

Challenge and career development

Challenge and career development is made up of:

- *career goals* - the individual decides where he wants to go;
- *career path planning* - with advice, the individual chooses the route he will take to achieve the goal;
- *training and job experience* - the organisation provides all the relevant experience and training to ensure that the individual continues to travel down the chosen route to the selected goal;
- *assessment and appraisal* - the organisation provides feedback as to the development of the individual measured against agreed expectation levels (see Chapter 5).

The major question is to decide who gets involved in the career development programmes. Three possibilities exist:

- *Fate:* The employee relies on pure chance to find the right job and allows fate to take him from job to job. Sometimes this works, but it needs a lot of luck. It is also the way to lose good employees.
- *The organisation:* The paternalistic organisation that consistently has the best interests of its employees at heart fulfils this role. There are very few such organisations around. Even where they exist, they run the risk of making the individual employee feel smothered by well meaning interference and as such will only attract a certain type of employee.
- *The employee:* The right way has to be for the employee to be the prime mover in career path planning. This need not work against the organisation; on the contrary, it will work in favour of the organisation that is able to offer its employees all they seek.

How to achieve employee-based career development planning

- Determine the career-based needs of the organisation, which really means know where the organisation is going and who it will need to get it there.
- Build career development planning into the appraisal system.
- Write the kind of job descriptions that define the skills, training and job experience required to do any job within the organisation.
- Encourage employees to understand themselves and build personal profiles. If they then compare their personal

assessments with the job descriptions, they will have built a route map for career development.

- Provide career development counselling, either from within the larger organisation or on an external basis for the small organisation.
- Encourage employees to manage their own careers, which will increase both their and the organisation's investment in their own performance.

A happy social environment with good team support

The philosophy of one large, happy, working family offers a great deal to commend it. Beware, however, for it will only attract one type of employee: those motivated by social needs (see Chapter 9). The organisation that provides such a working environment is relying on the incentive properties of groups to produce the chosen environment (see Chapter 7).

There is no better job to be found

Beware the demotivational aspects of the individual who is trapped in a job, once the very pinnacle of his career goals, which is now perceived to be a threatening trap. Wanting a job is one thing; being trapped in a job to which there is no equal is a restriction. However good the job, even though it may continue to provide the motivational goals, the threat of no longer being able to achieve the freedom of choice can cause poor performance.

The Peter Principle

Promotion to the level of one's own incompetence still operates. If the individual perceives that level of incompetence, he may well opt to stay in the organisation that has allowed the situation to come about. The theory is that eventually everyone will reach the level of their own incompetence and there they will stay. The answers are to:

- promote through the level of incompetence in the belief that the individual can rise above the level;
- train at an early stage to continually move back the level of incompetence;
- practise the art of demotion and sideways moves to ensure that the individual who reaches his level of incompetence is given another opportunity at a lower or parallel level within the organisation.

Promotion before recruitment

In an organisation that has effective career development planning, promotion will be the natural solution to the vacancy problem. To aid such promotion, appraisal systems should be kept (see Chapter 6). These should be designed to understand the in-depth skills of the individual and to look out for the unused potential that may be there. Always keep records of the ancillary skills of your employees: who speaks the foreign languages, who has basic computer knowledge; who understands the skills of clients and customers; who has had experiences in personal life or education that can lead them to a greater understanding of areas they might otherwise be unable to deal with.

Getting someone back

Occasionally, a really good employee will leave the organisation. Perhaps the next step up the ladder is just not visible within his time scale, perhaps he needs the opportunity to grow outside the confines of his training base. Whatever the reason, make sure that the lines of communication remain open. The golden rule is never to allow anyone to depart under a cloud of disappointment or misjudgement. At the very least, they will be taking bad memories of their experiences to the outside world, where they may damage your image.

People who return to organisations with external experiences are likely to be able to see the organisation more clearly. They are the ones to mastermind the introduction of change and development within such organisations. So how do you get them back?

- *Never lose touch:* Make and keep contact at the traditional times of the year. Consider old employee gatherings from time to time.
- *Tell people you would like them to return:* Ring them up and invite them back when the vacancy occurs. Very few have such high opinions of themselves that they would automatically assume that return is what you want.
- *Make sure people understand when they leave that you would be willing to see them back in the future:* Counsel them on leaving. Get their opinions on what is right and what is wrong with the organisation, and listen to what they say (the exit

interview). Never sulk or turn sour because someone has chosen to go. Keep it pleasant and smiling up to the end. Make them feel sad to be going.

Changing the job to match the existing people

So many organisations seem to feel that once the job is designed its outline is sacrosanct. Here is where the lesson can be learned from the smaller organisation. Use the people within the team to achieve the tasks set by the organisation. Attack every situation from the point of view of the resources, human and otherwise, that are known to exist.

If you build a team that feels like a team, thinks like a team and works like a team, the members will change the job to match their own perceived resources.

Feel like a team
People feel like members of a team if they are treated as a team. Consult with them, ask their opinions, tell them the full facts of the situation and listen to what they have to say. Listen to ideas from the members of the team and use other members to develop the ideas to the full.

Think like a team
Once the team spirit is there, people will have the capacity for thinking as a team. To encourage this, always set the task in context, always give them the full criteria to be considered and report back the final outcome so that they can measure their performance in future.

Work like a team
People who think and feel like a team will forget their individual roles and start to work as members of a team who can see the outcome of their joint actions. To encourage this, reward the team as a team. Treat them to team debriefings and give praise to the team as a whole. Try not to single out the individual, unless a particularly high level of performance is there to merit praise. Always wait for the whole team to be there before you begin a briefing session.

Chapter 5
Appraisal

Why appraisal?

The very best way to ensure that people do the tasks required of them to the best of their ability is to make sure that they know what their best is. Very few people are in fact good judges of their own efforts. Appraisal means that the individual is given feedback against which he can measure his future performance. Every task that is undertaken should result in such feedback. Part of good leadership is to ensure that the team and the individual are aware of how the task has been concluded and what the value of their contribution was. However, there remains a need for a formal six-monthly appraisal (see example at end of chapter) with each employee to:

- review progress and establish priorities;
- resolve any problems;
- discuss the individual's future potential and training needs.

At the end of the appraisal interview, the appraisee should be able to answer the questions:

- How am I doing?
- Where am I going?
- What can I do to improve?

What is appraisal?

Appraisal is not:

- the manager telling the employee what he did wrong;
- a secret report that the employee never sees;
- another name for a disciplinary interview;
- an attack on the employee or a character assassination;
- a salary discussion.

Appraisal is, however:

- a two-way discussion between interested parties;
- an open matter that both appraiser and appraisee sign;
- a plan for the future;
- a constructive criticism of the past;
- a meeting without emotions involved.

Planning the appraisal interview

Preparation

- Read the case history in advance.
- Discuss the appraisee with colleagues to get a full opinion.
- Fill in the appraisal form.
- Read the report from the last appraisal session.
- Send the completed appraisal report to the appraisee for his consideration so that he can prepare for the meeting too.

Organising the interview

- Fix a mutually convenient time.
- Do not plan more than four appraisal interviews in one day.
- Make sure the interviewee understands how the interview will be conducted and what it means.
- Prepare the interview room. Ensure that there are no interruptions.
- Clear the air of any previous aggravations before commencing the interview.

Conducting the interview

- Use the appraisal form as a trigger to discussion, not as a dissection document.
- Try to put yourself in the appraisee's shoes.
- Listen with an open mind to what is said.
- Don't argue.
- Don't allow the conversation to drift to unrelated subjects.
- Keep your language clear and free from misinterpretation.

- Don't duck the issue if something difficult has to be said.
- Don't rely on your memory.
- Make sure the interview is a two-way discussion.

Planning action

- Plan how to use a person's strengths in the future.
- Discuss how to achieve any improvements required.
- Determine how the appraisee sees his development.

Reporting the interview

- Make sure that both parties fill in and sign the appraisal form.
- Give a copy to the appraisee.
- File a copy for next time.

Golden rules for conducting the appraisal interview

1. Create a relaxed atmosphere.
2. State the objectives of the exercise.
3. Use open-ended questions to get discussion going: What was the most interesting task you had to do in the last six months? Where do you think you achieved most successes last year? How do you feel you handled . . . . ? What areas of your work would you say require more attention? What extra help do you need to improve in those areas? What do you think you need to learn now to develop the job further?
4. Probe if details are missed or the appraisee speaks in generalities.
5. Ensure you review all key areas of the job.
6. Let your views be clearly known to the appraisee.
7. Praise for work well done.
8. Point out areas for improvement and explain why.
9. Demonstrate how you think improvement can be achieved.
10. Encourage.
11. Summarise from time to time.
12. Discuss future training needs and development.
13. Set action plans.
14. End on a positive note.

Six-monthly appraisal form

The purpose of appraisal is to review ability and progress to date. In the light of that review, all involved parties should agree on future developments and expectations, including training and experience requirements.

Technical

Work type 1   *Level guide**
Has a satisfactory standard been consistently achieved?

1   2   3   4   5   6

Target not   Target totally
achieved   achieved

Work type 2   *Level guide**
Has a satisfactory standard been consistently achieved?

6   5   4   3   2   1

Target not   Target totally
achieved   achieved

Work type 3   *Level guide**
Has a satisfactory standard been consistently achieved?

1   2   3   4   5   6

Target not   Target totally
achieved   achieved

Work type 4   *Level guide**
Has a satisfactory standard been consistently achieved?

6   5   4   3   2   1

Target not   Target totally
achieved   achieved

---

* Level guide = level of expertise expected from individual concerned. This would possibly be linked to rank length of service, or experience.

Personal skills

Communication   *Level guide**

Has a satisfactory standard of achievement been consistently maintained?

| 6 | 5 | 4 | 3 | 2 | 1 |

Target not   Target totally
achieved   achieved

Performance   *Level guide**

Has a satisfactory level of effort been maintained?

| 6 | 5 | 4 | 3 | 2 | 1 |

Target not   Target totally
achieved   achieved

Projection   *Level guide**

Has a satisfactory standard been consistently achieved?

| 1 | 2 | 3 | 4 | 5 | 6 |

Target not   Target totally
achieved   achieved

Man management   *Level guide**

Has a satisfactory standard been consistently achieved?

| 1 | 2 | 3 | 4 | 5 | 6 |

Target not   Target totally
achieved   achieved

---

* Level guide = level of expertise expected from individual concerned. This would possibly be linked to rank length of service, or experience.

Exception report

_____
_____
_____
_____

Job satisfaction
What level of job satisfaction have you experienced to date?

Low					High
1	2	3	4	5	6

Future plans
What targets should you try to meet in the next 12 months?

_____
_____
_____
_____

Which of those targets should be achieved within six months and
subjected to rolling review at the next assessment?

_____
_____
_____
_____

What training is needed?
Reported to _____

On the job training

_____
_____

Training sessions

_____
_____

Signed _____ Date _____

Appraiser _____ Appraisee _____

Appraisal preparation for the appraisee

The purpose of this form is to help the appraisee to prepare for appraisal, so that the meeting can be as meaningful as possible. The answers may well not be shown to the appraiser; the form is merely to help the appraisee to think clearly.

What particular parts of the job interest me most?

_____

_____

What particular parts interest me least?

_____

_____

How have I carried out the main tasks I am responsible for?

_____

_____

Which tasks could have been performed more effectively, and how?

_____

_____

What is preventing me from being more effective in these areas?

_____

_____

What tasks have I performed particularly well?

_____

_____

What areas are unclear in my job?

_____

_____

What extra help or guidance would I like to receive?

_____

_____

Where do I want to be in five years' time?

_____

_____

Chapter 6
Discipline

The disciplinary interview

It is essential that standards and discipline are maintained within an office environment. From time to time, it will be necessary to conduct a disciplinary interview. Occasionally, that disciplinary interview will be part of the process of dismissal. Because of employment legislation, the disciplinary procedure should:

- be in writing;
- specify to whom it applies;
- provide for matters to be dealt with quickly;
- indicate the disciplinary actions that may be taken;
- specify the levels of management who have the authority to take disciplinary action;
- provide for individuals to be informed of complaints against them;
- give individuals the right to be accompanied by a trade union representative or a fellow employee of their choice;
- ensure that, except for gross misconduct, no employees are dismissed for a first breach of discipline;
- ensure that disciplinary action is not taken until the case has been carefully investigated;
- ensure that individuals are given an explanation of any penalty imposed;
- provide a right of appeal and specify the procedure to be followed.

Conducting the interview

A disciplinary interview is all about the future and not a moan about the past. It must never be conducted in the heat of the moment.

Before the interview

- Take time to cool down.
- Establish the gap between real and expected performance:
  — Check the facts about the individual's performance.
  — Check the required performance.
  — Establish the discrepancy.
- Warn the disciplinee.

At the interview

- Explain the gap and the required performance, and show where the disciplinee's performance falls short.
- Explore the reasons for the gap:
  — Ask why the disciplinee has behaved as he did.
  — Listen to the reply.
  — Use open-ended questions such as who?, what?, why?, how?, where?, when?
  — Don't accept generalisations for answers.
  — Don't argue.
  — Be firm.
  — Be fair.
- Consider the following:
  — Is the problem just a way of getting attention?
  — Does the person need training or help?
  — Is there a personal cause?
  — Are the rules wrong?
  — Is conflict or personality clash the real cause?
  — Have the organisation's requirements been communicated properly in the first instance?
  — Is this really a matter for discipline?
- Eliminate the gap:
  — Agree what is wrong.
  — Set realistic new targets.
  — Fix review date.

After the interview

- Write a report.

Dealing with the difficult

When people are subjected to complaint and discipline, they act in different ways. There is, however, an underlying theme to the reactions of someone about to be disciplined and that theme of reaction is based in the individual's natural response to fear. Some people respond to fear by becoming aggressive, fighting and arguing; others become defensive, and a final group withdraw into their shells and refuse to acknowledge the problem. None of these reactions is easy to deal with. In part, they may trigger unsatisfactory reactions in the disciplinarian, thereby making the session even harder to conduct.

Difficult people can be categorised into certain characters: each has his own idiosyncrasy and needs to be handled accordingly:

- *The artful dodger:*
  This person tries to avoid the issue by bringing up irrelevant points.
  Make sure your facts are right and stick to them.
  Keep bringing him back to the point.
  Don't let unrelated matters creep into the conversation.
- *The injured innocent:*
  Defensive systems mean that nothing can possibly have been his fault.
  Make sure your facts are right and stick to them.
  Ignore the assumed injured innocence.
  Deliberately take the wind out of his sails.
- *The compulsive confessor:*
  If a problem arises, this character will always accept blame, but not responsibility.
  Don't accept confession as contrition.
  Don't let him go until an improvement plan is agreed.
  Stay firm.
- *The buck passer:*
  It is always someone else who should be blamed.
  Make sure your facts are right and stick to them.
  The buck stops here, what are you going to do about it?
- *The barrack room lawyer:*
  Some of these characters actually carry legal handbooks, others just rely on the office procedures manual. Either way, they know their facts and are intent on talking you out of your viewpoint.
  Let him talk himself out.
  Listen using non-directive techniques.
  Know your facts and stick to them.
  Refuse to be sidetracked.

How to Solve Your People Problems

- *The sly fox:*
  This character is a mix of silent withdrawal and defensiveness.
  The longer he stays silent, the more talking you will do and the
  more likely you are to weaken your case.
  Make him do some of the talking.
  Use open-ended questions and wait for the answers.
  Know your facts and prepare well.
  If he finds a weakness, don't allow it to dominate the
  conversation.
  Don't become defensive.
- *The professional weeper:*
  This person can shed tears at the drop of a hat. Tears are always
  thought to be an indication that the other party is being
  excessively cruel and tend to draw sympathy to the weeper. The
  professional knows this and relies on particularly the male fear
  of tears.
  Have paper tissues available, but don't weaken.
  Keep the interview factual.
  Point out that the matter is not personal.
  Be kind but firm.
  Try to make him laugh.
- *The compulsive resigner:*
  This person solves everything by stamping a foot. Anger in this
  case is expressed in the threat of resignation. The last thing
  this person wants is for the threat of resignation to be taken up.
  Don't back down.
  Offer to accept the resignation indicating what a shame it will
  be.
  Be firm and friendly.
  Offer to discuss his employment at a later date when everyone
  is calmer.
- *The depressive:*
  Some people give in to depression very easily. It is another
  version of tears and intended to extract full sympathy.
  Point out that you believe they are capable of the task, they just
  need some help.
  Help them to help themselves.
  Don't make too many allowances.
  Be firm.
  State clearly your required standards and by when you expect
  them to be achieved.

- *The counter-attacker:*
  This one is ready for a fight at any time. If you let the discipline turn into any kind of argument, he will have won and what's more he will in all probability win the argument too.
  Don't argue - it takes two to fight.
  Listen in silence.
  Then return to the subject.
  Keep off personal levels.
  Ignore all slights on your character.
  Be firm and be fair.

Grievances and personal problems

If it is really a grievance or personal problem and not a matter for discipline at all, you should act as follows.

Personal problems
- Be sympathetic, but be careful.
- Don't try to solve people's problems for them. You won't succeed and you'll get all the blame.
- Show them how they can solve problems themselves.
- Explain to the other staff any concession you give.

Grievances
- If it is possible, try to resolve the problem on the spot.
- If that is not possible, go away and think it over, but set a comeback date.
- Explain that you feel it is a pity that the person did not come to see you earlier.
- Remind him of the grievance procedure.
- Learn from your own mistakes.
- Be approachable.

Chapter 7
Supervision

People in groups

Types of group
There are two types of group to be found in the working
environment: formal and informal. Formal groups are those set up
by the organisation; those over which the organisation has most
control and for whose membership-based problems it has only
itself to blame. Informal groups are those set up by the individuals
themselves. It is important to realise that human beings need
groups. What they are not given, they will provide for themselves.

People need groups
People need groups because man is not the lone hunter, but rather
a gregarious animal who needs the support of others. There are six
common reasons behind the need for groups.

Security
A group offers protection from real and imagined external threats.
In the office environment, this is likely to be the threat of making a
mistake. One of the principal reasons for partnerships is always
given as the achievement of a broader base of knowledge, which
loosely translates as protection from mistakes. The supportive
group helps, comforts and encourages.

The effective office group able to answer this need will have a
mix of abilities and levels of knowledge among its members, so
that within the group each person can find someone to whom they
can relate.

Never forget that some members of the group may be members
of other groups too. For example, in an office-based subject group,
the senior member may be the Production Director, who is also a
member of the group known as the Board of Directors.

Social needs
People need to interact with others and develop meaningful relationships; they need friendship. The effective organisation-based group will be such that friendships can be encouraged within it. Thus, when allocating people to existing groups, it is worth considering the present composition of the group and how the newcomer will fit into it. In the right group, he will make friends and develop a sense of loyalty; in the wrong group, he will rebel and cause a potential backlash of demotivation among the other members. Remember the stages of socialisation and individualisation when an employee joins an organisation - these apply equally to the transfer to a new group.

Self-esteem needs
People take a great deal of pride in being associated with groups that they consider to be prestigious. Encouraging membership of such groups, by encouraging training and active participation, will motivate the self-esteem needs of the individual.

Within the organisation, it is important to establish equally prestigious groups - the 'senior secretaries', for example, or the 'tax discussion group' - groups that indicate that the members have achieved a special status. Such groups motivate the existing membership and those who are striving for membership equally.

Economics
People often associate with groups to pursue their own economic interest. Membership of a trade union is one example of the economic use of groups. Members believe that, banded together, they are best able to make sure that they get equal and fair treatment. It may mean that a group of staff gather together to fight for better pay and conditions.

It is essential in the organisation to recognise the need for economic-based groups. You must accept their nature and use them, not as a negotiating tool, but as an advisory group, able to contribute to the wellbeing of the organisation and its staff generally. You must admit their grievances, if they truly exist, but encourage them to take the positive approach, which may lead to the resolution of the problem. Staff consultative groups are one example of just such a use of the economic-based group need.

Group goals

Groups often get together because they have a single aim and that aim is best pursued together. United we stand, divided we fall. Conservancy groups fall into this category.

Within the organisation, it is as well to accept that people will want to form groups of this type, perhaps with a sporting or pastime-orientated activity in mind. Encouragement of such groups will enhance the caring image of the organisation.

Group goals can also be work-orientated; for example, to get a task completed within a time limit, particularly if there are challenges such as problems in the way.

Proximity

People who work together tend to form temporary groups, and when they leave the organisation they go to join another temporary group, retaining no connection with the first group.

In the organisation you must make use of this tendency to your own ends. If a group is constantly heard chattering and not working, that is a temporary group that should not have been allowed to form. Now is the time to try to change its pattern without being seen to destroy the group. Attack from without will only cause the group to knot more tightly together. Proximity groups are the least strong in their reasons for grouping, so they are the easiest to alter, but even that must be done with care. If the group is large, split them up into working units, pointing out that this will give them better working conditions and more autonomy. Encourage them to gather together at social periods instead.

The development of groups

There are four distinct development stages of the group:

- forming;
- storming;
- norming;
- performing.

Forming - the undeveloped team

Testing and establishing rules

At this stage, members try to discover the pattern of behaviour that will be acceptable to the group. For groups without written rules, new members have to depend on the existing members to help them understand and conform. Thus, the existence of written rules will help this stage of the group formation.

Revolutionary or awkward members of a new group will try at this stage of development to force behaviour patterns to one or another extreme. If the reactionary individual has a strong personality and leadership ability, it may be that the new group takes on a totally unexpected and undesirable form. Setting written rules will help to prevent this. If written rules seem too formal, setting the group a task and the responsibility to solve it may well have the same effect as written rules. It will serve to help them get their priorities right, eg office procedures manual.

Storming - the experimenting team
Intra-group conflict
A high degree of intra-group conflict can be expected as members compete for roles within the group. These conflicts are part of the development of the group and should not be restricted. On the other hand, however, the group that is fighting a small war within itself will not be an effective group. If too much scope is allowed for intra-group conflict, the right leader may not emerge and the group may split and divide.

In selecting a leader for a group, it is essential to realise that this stage of formation exists and to be aware of the strength that the leader will need to show. Leadership training is the essential aid to the smooth formation of groups through the storming stage of development.

Norming - the consolidating team
Development of group cohesion
Once roles have been established, group members settle down and develop a sense of loyalty to the group. This is the stage at which the group can develop loyalties to the organisation far stronger than the individual members of the group have to the same organisation. Encourage group loyalty to the organisation, it will prevent inter-departmental wars, which themselves can have terrible effects. Consider the marketing and sales group that is so loyal to itself that it wages a war on production - where is the organisation in that situation?

Performing - the mature team
Functional role relatedness

Once established, the group settles down to achieving its aims. A division of tasks is made among members of the group, taking advantage of specialist knowledge. This final stage of performing continues throughout the life of the group and individuals can now be placed within the group to help the development of that group.

Keeping the group together

Motive base for attraction

The needs of the individual are the primary reasons why he joined the group in the first place. If the group continues to satisfy his needs, he will continue his membership. Thus, a group must be monitored continually for its satisfaction of the changing and developing needs of its members.

Incentive properties of groups and teams

Prestige

The prestige of membership, the goals for the group and the personal characteristics of other group members are all reasons why an individual stays within a group. Equally, they may be reasons why he chooses to leave it. It is therefore important for the group to remain true to its stated objectives and membership aims and not to change significantly. Where change is needed, it is wiser to change the individual membership mix rather than the group itself.

Expectancy about outcomes

If members believe in the group and its ability to achieve its aims, they will remain in the group. If they lose faith in the group and its ability to achieve its aims, they will leave the group. If a group is given an unrealistic goal, it will become frustrated, demotivated and split up. Any goal should be presented to the group with achievement stages clearly marked along the path so that the group can monitor its own progress. Never leave a group to a task without seeking feedback, and without active monitoring of that feedback.

Comparison level
The membership of one group is compared and contrasted with membership of another; the best group wins. In the organisation that has both set up formal groups and encouraged the formation of informal groups, this can be a very important factor. The informal groups must not be allowed to appear more attractive than the formal groups as the members will change their allegiance. Natural competition, however, in the form of sporting matches or achievement goals, should be encouraged as the success of one group can stimulate the further achievements of another group.

The problems with groups

From time to time, the very existence of a group within the organisation seems to bring about problems:

- proximity groups;
- wrong or contradictory group goals;
- prolonged storming;
- over-mature and under-performing groups, ie too little change;
- untrained or ineffective leadership.

The first four problems can be solved with effective supervision. The fifth is simply a need for the right leader or supervisor to be taught the best way to lead the group.

Supervision

In a general management context, the title 'supervisor' usually indicates someone who is on the first level of promotion from the general post of clerk, which is a misuse of the term. The job of supervision is to lead and control a group as a member of that group, thus performing part of the responsibilities delegated downwards from the next level of hierarchy within the organisation. All management roles have supervisory responsibilities; all leaders need to be good supervisors too.

Choosing a supervisor
It is the job of the next level up to choose a supervisor for any group. That choice must be made with great care. Too many mistakes are made when no one has made sure that the selected individual is ready for the role and has had time to consider it. Promote too early and you may ruin someone's chances for growth for a long time.

Promote without training and you will not be rewarded with effective work, but rather with a demotivated supervisor and a frustrated and demotivated group. Here are some factors that should be considered:

- *Timing:* Choose the supervisor at the right moment in his or her career path.
- *Communicate:*
  — Explain carefully the role to be undertaken and make sure the supervisor has adequate knowledge.
  — Make sure those who work for the supervisor understand the role.
  — Make the scope and limits of the supervisor's responsibilities clear.
  — Make reporting responsibilities clear.
  — Ensure that the supervisor understands and communicates the team's objectives effectively.
- *Loyalty:* Insist on total loyalty both to the organisation and the team.
- *Train:* Give the supervisor central guidance and support.
- *Delegate:* Set aside regular time slots for meetings and feedback sessions.

Supervising techniques
The job of supervision can be broken down into six areas:

- leadership;
- communication;
- training;
- umpiring;
- counselling;
- worker member of the team.

Leadership
Being in charge of other people means a change of status. The supervisor is still responsible for his own work, but now he has the additional responsibility of overseeing the work of others. The staff working for him now look to him for leadership and guidance. The supervisor is the leader of a team, which will become just what the supervisor makes it.

Leadership checklist
- Delegate the workload sensibly and fairly.
- Keep the team committed to the job, both by guidance and example.
- Represent the organisation fairly and with loyalty.
- Stand up for your own team.
- Face problems as they arise; don't back away from them.

Communication

Being a good leader means being a good communicator. A good communicator takes time to say clearly and accurately what the team needs to know. It means stopping from time to time to ask if they understand what is required of them. It means being a good listener. An effective communicator saves time by taking time to put thought and effort into communications.

Communication checklist
- Make sure the team know what they have to do and why they have to do it.
- Discuss regularly how the team tackles a task, so that they can express thoughts and ideas.
- Tell the managers how things are going.
- Pass on the ideas and opinions of your team.
- Keep in touch with peer groups.
- Don't tell tales on the team.

Training

Being in charge of junior staff means having some responsibility for ensuring that they are trained to do the job required of them.

Training checklist
- Make sure you understand completely the task that each member of the team has to undertake.
- Make sure each member of the team understands fully the tasks he has to do.
- Never be afraid to learn from the team.

Umpiring

Where two or more people are gathered together there is bound to be a conflict. Sometimes things simply go wrong; sometimes it is human nature that causes the conflict. Whatever the cause it is the job of the supervisor to make sure that the situation is returned to normal as soon as possible.

How to Solve Your People Problems

Umpiring checklist
- Make sure every member of the team pulls his own weight.
- If there is a breach of discipline *never* bawl out the offending party in front of others.
- Always let both sides state their case.
- Try to find out why problems occur.
- Give clear warning of any disciplinary steps you intend to take.
- Stay within employment law.
- If the problem is too difficult, refer it upwards.
- Be impartial and fair at all times.

Counselling
The leader of the team must always be prepared for people to come seeking advice. If they don't come for advice, the leader should worry; it means they are going elsewhere and the leadership role is being undermined. Giving advice is not easy. No one expects you to know all, but you should know where to go to find the information and advice needed.

Counselling checklist
- Take a personal interest in each member of the team.
- Find out what makes each member tick.
- Be prepared to help and give advice when it is needed.
- Be a good active listener.
- Take the initiative in introducing members of the team to services and facts that may help them.
- When someone asks for advice always give the facts, even if they are unpalatable.
- Keep counselling confidential, at all times.
- Remember you cannot solve someone else's problem; all you can do is show him how to solve it himself.

Worker member of the team
Being in charge of a team does not mean you can delegate all the work and simply sit back and watch. The supervisor must pull his weight too. The role of supervision simply means that you keep an eye on the work of others while still doing your own share of the workload.

Membership checklist
- Delegate, but keep a fair share of the work for yourself.
- Make sure your standards set an example to others.
- Give credit where it is due.
- Never forget you are responsible for the whole team's output.

Chapter 8
Delegation

The art of delegating

Delegation is the art of getting a job done by the person best able to do it in the time available. It involves briefing someone else on aspects of your own job and handing on aspects of that job to him. Many people fail to delegate sufficiently; usually for one of the following reasons.

Risk
All delegation involves risk. As you can't avoid it, accept it and make sure that the minimum risk is taken.

- Plan delegation.
- Demonstrate faith in the delegatee.
- Explain how to do the task and get feedback.
- No risk; no growth.

Letting go
At some stage, you will have to let someone else do your favourite task. Vocational hobbies are all very well but they must not take up more than 5 per cent of your working time.

- Plan your time.
- Reward yourself with 5 per cent vocational hobbies.
- The technical term is *growing up*.

Sitting and thinking is also working
Some people seem to believe that unless they are rushing around or pushing paper at a rate of knots they are not working. This is not true.

- Thinking before doing saves time.
- Read the instructions before starting to use the equipment.

Patience

All delegation requires patience. Nobody does a new task for the first time at the speed the delegator hoped for. Too fast may mean too many mistakes.

- Expect to take time - plan for it.
- Explain fully.
- Explain in digestible chunks.
- Get feedback.

Losing control

If you think you can only remain on top of the job if you touch everything that goes through the office, you are wrong. That is remaining close to the job, too close to see the wood for the trees, and that is losing control. Control of the job means standing back and reviewing all that is done.

- Stand back and watch.
- Use your new knowledge to change and adapt for the better.

Handing on the job

It does mean handing on part of the job; it does not mean losing the job. It might mean more time to take over a new and more interesting job.

- You must delegate power.
- You must delegate authority.
- You cannot delegate responsibility.
- Grow into the next job up the line.

Nobody does it like you do

Of course, they won't do it the same way as you do, but if you:

- train
- explain
- monitor

they will do it as well as it needs to be done.

The delegation plan: What to delegate and to whom

No one can make the decision for you, but if you make the decision using the following rules, you'll make the right decision:

Write a plan
- Set out the main objectives of your job.
- Conduct a time audit (brief) for the last month.
- List your actual activities compared with the objectives.

Decide what can be delegated
- List what cannot be delegated:
    — tasks beyond the skills of others
    — confidential and security matters
    — disciplinary matters.
- List the routine tasks.
- List the time-consuming tasks.

Decide to whom you will delegate
- Who has time?
- Who is ready for new challenges?
- What training will be needed?

Delegate the task
- Define the task.
- Establish the problems and pitfalls of the task.
- Define any additional authority needed.
- Establish the authority.
- Explain the task and its pitfalls and good points.
- Go through the task with the delegatee.
- Watch the delegatee go through the task.
- Set report back targets.
- Monitor.

On-the-job training

Never be tempted to gloss over the training part of the act of delegation. If the team does not understand how to complete a task, the leader/delegater will simply end up clearing up the subsequent problems or taking all the blame for a task that has been improperly completed.

Much of the time it is the lack of good communication and understanding that causes the tuition failures. You need to have patience to save yourself time in the long run. Even if the task you need to explain seems completely straightforward, remember that it is new and different to someone else.

Preparation is essential in giving any effective training:

- Who is going to learn?
- What are they going to learn?
- What equipment do you need to teach them?
- How long will it take you to pass on your knowledge?

Without asking yourself these four questions and giving yourself considered replies, you cannot give effective on-the-job training. Start to train the team by planning the session.

How people learn

In order to teach effectively, you need to understand how people learn, as follows:

- concentration curve;
- retention curve;
- what senses they learn with;
- the way information is received and assimilated.

Concentration curve

Most people cannot concentrate totally on one subject for longer than 45 minutes. Even that is rather a long time to spend on one subject. People find concentration easier at different periods of the day. It is less easy to concentrate after a large meal, or if they are clockwatching for an expected event.

Figure 1 shows concentration patterns for an average day. The patterns are typical whether or not the person concerned is best in the morning or the afternoon, although there is no doubt that 'larks' and 'owls' do concentrate differently in the centre core of the day.

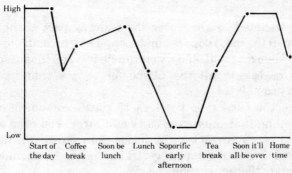

Figure 1. *How people concentrate*

Retention curve

People learn in short spurts; breaks within a learning period ensure that a higher point of recall is achieved. If a two-hour learning period is needed, then so are three breaks at half-hourly intervals.

Over a two-hour learning period, the following retention patterns can be achieved:

- Two hours with three half-hourly breaks: 75 per cent.
- Two hours with no breaks: 50 per cent average.
- Two hours with no breaks as part of a longer period: between 50 per cent and 30 per cent.

See Figure 2 for details of the retention curve.

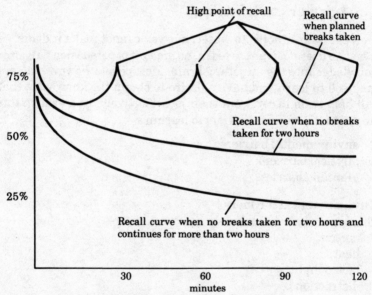

Figure 2. *How people remember*

Learning with the senses

The human animal communicates through the five senses as follows:

- Sight: 75 per cent.
- Hearing: 13 per cent.
- Touch, taste and smell: 12 per cent.

Individuals will recall 10 per cent of what they hear after three days; 20 per cent of what they see after three days; and 65 per cent of what they see and hear after three days. Thus, to extend retention, use visual effect.

The way information is received and assimilated

- The task always needs to be set in context. No task can be effectively completed without full understanding of how it fits into the job as a whole.
- The job needs to be broken down into units. Small chunks of the job need to be explained at a time. The trainee needs to master each small chunk before he passes on to the next.
- The trainee needs to practise what he has been taught.

The barriers to learning

'You can take a horse to water, but you cannot make it drink.' If someone does not want to learn, no amount of persuasion will force knowledge into the unwilling brain. Most people, however, accept the need to learn and have a desire to obtain the knowledge that will help them to carry out their jobs effectively. But, even in this situation, there exist barriers to learning:

- environmental barriers;
- physical barriers;
- planning barriers;

Environmental barriers

This type of barrier includes:

- noise;
- heat;
- lack of light;
- distractions.

In other words, any kind of external interference may stop the individual's learning process. Make sure as few as possible of the barriers are present.

Physical barriers

These include:

- colour blindness;
- poor eyesight;
- deafness;
- lack of understanding of English.

If the trainee is suffering from one of these physical barriers, he needs to be helped. You need to know enough about the trainee to be aware of his problems so that you can show him how to compensate. For example:

- explain without the use of colour keys;
- speak slowly;
- enunciate clearly.

Be prepared to give remedial advice; it's all part of counselling. For example:

- the name of an optician;
- an English language course.

Never ignore the physical barriers because you are too embarrassed to mention them. It is kinder and better management practice to point them out in a one-to-one interview and offer constructive help.

Planning barriers
These barriers include:

- not allowing enough time for the training session;
- not giving the trainee enough warning of the session;
- not planning for feedback sessions.

You must plan the session to make sure that no one's time is wasted. People need to know what is going to happen to them - you want the full concentration of the trainee, so you want him to be in the right receptive mood. Not allowing enough time for the session will simply mean that it is rushed and as a result less effective. Lack of feedback sessions will simply mean that you do not get a chance to correct minor misunderstandings before they become major behaviour patterns.

Why people learn

People learn to satisfy all sorts of needs within them. Key direct learning needs may be:

- the desire to win;
- the search for promotion and challenge;
- the longing for something new;

- satisfaction of a personal goal;
- monetary reward;
- status reward;
- responsibility reward.

The trick is to spot the right manifest need and use it to encourage and help stimulate the learning process.

Motivation
People are motivated by:

- achievement
- recognition
- work itself
- responsibility
- advancement

provided these stimulants are there in the right amount and correctly offered. Equally, the lack of these items can demotivate the individual. Make sure the training enhances the motivating factors.

Encouragement
At times, even the most able find learning hard. Anyone tackling a new task feels foolish. Most are afraid of making a mistake. Such factors can make the trainee appear slow and clumsy. Simple encouragement helps.

Treat mistakes as an opportunity to learn. Those who do the task perfectly only learn how to do the task perfectly; those who make mistakes learn:

- how to do the task;
- how to put right mistakes;
- how mistakes occur;
- not to make mistakes again.

Feedback and montoring
Effective training requires receptive feedback and monitoring.

- Take time to answer questions.
- Don't sound exasperated.
- But don't take over the task for the nervous trainee.

Training hints

Watch your language
- Avoid unusual or long words.
- Avoid jargon unless you have explained it first, or it is well understood and essential to the job.
- Avoid emotional phrases such as 'This is child's play', 'Anyone could do this' and 'It's so simple'. The implication is that if you can't do it first time, you must be thick, and that puts pressure on the trainee.
- Use factual words.
- Refer back to earlier training sessions.

Use questions
Questions make sure that the trainee:

- is listening;
- has understood;
- is encouraged to think through the approach to the task himself;
- still retains earlier knowledge and experience;
- is ready to learn further.

Make sure the questions are:

- fair and relevant;
- not easy to guess;
- require full answers, not just yes or no;
- test knowledge.

Try to use open-ended questions, as these allow the trainee to explain all he understands and to explore his own knowledge.

Simple rules of explaining
- Get the training material in the right order.
- Know the trainee.
- Link the training to the trainee's existing knowledge.
- Concentrate on positive instructions.
- Give the trainee feedback on his progress.
- Allow the trainee time to practise.
- Top up the training from time to time.

How to Solve Your People Problems

The trainer's checklist

Once you have given a piece of on-the-job training, sit back and assess your own efforts. The only way to improve as a trainer is to ensure that you learn from your own efforts. Did you:

- prepare well?
- put the job into context?
- warn the trainee what to expect?
- break down the job into digestible chunks?
- put over the training in the right sequence?
- bring out special or key points?
- show confidence and enthusiasm?
- get and maintain the trainee's interest?
- get the trainee to participate?
- ask the right questions?
- make proper use of equipment and written notes?
- use your own notes?
- follow up your instructions to evaluate effectiveness?
- make sure the trainee knew how he was getting on?
- ensure that the trainee's final performance was up to standard?

Chapter 9
Motivation

Demotivation factors

You probably know the effect demotivated people can have on the success of an organisation. Indeed, demotivation seems to spread like some kind of wet rot; once one person is unhappy they upset a few around them and the whole department turns into an unhappy workforce.

The demotivators
What makes them unhappy in the first place? Here are some causes:

- salary;
- job security;
- personal life;
- working conditions;
- status;
- company policies and administration;
- supervision;
- inter-personal relations with peer groups and subordinates.

Salary
If the salary is wrong, everything is wrong. The wrong salary is usually too low a salary. Once the salary level is perceived to be lower than that available for the same job elsewhere, the individual becomes dissatisfied. Put the salary right and no more will be said. Pay too high a salary, either as a reward or as a method of making sure you don't lose key staff, and you'll find the same level of demotivation returning. Indeed, too high a salary can have an almost worse effect than too low a salary.

Consider the case of the expatriate who would like to come home, but simply cannot afford in the UK to have the kind of lifestyle to which he has become accustomed. Or the case of the individual who was under-qualified for his job, but nevertheless promoted on the grounds that his experience was so valuable that the organisation would be the poorer without him. Eventually, he decided to look for a new job, only to find that all he was offered was two-thirds of his present salary and a car of much reduced standard. He left his job search a frustrated and demotivated man, and the response of his employers to increase his salary only made the matter worse.

Money demotivates when it is wrong, either because it is perceived to be too low or too high a salary.

Job security

When people are unsure about the likely continuation of their job, they become insecure and regress to deficiency needs (see Chapter 10). One way of describing demotivation is to say that the individual is no longer motivated by the need he apparently demonstrated beforehand.

People who are unsure about the continuation of their job usually take steps to ensure that another job will be there should they need it. As a result of job insecurity, the best people leave and the ones who cannot find another job stay and demotivate others. If there is total job security, however, there is no matching upswing in effort or motivation; people just ignore the security factor and get on with the job.

Personal life

When personal life and happiness go wrong, they affect the whole balance of an individual's approach, and inevitably affect work. Consider the individual who is trying to sell one house and move to another. Given the legal system in England and Wales, he is bound to have delays and problems: Will the sale go through? Will the mortgage be granted? When will the papers be signed? Will a bridging loan be necessary? For long periods of the working day, these problems fill his mind rather than the problems that relate to his work. Give him time to solve his personal problems and the level of work will return to normal once the personal problems are out of the way.

Conversely, the individual whose private life is going particularly well is unlikely to show that happiness in his efforts at work. Indeed, the preoccupation with happiness may result in less time being devoted to work and more to day-dreaming.

Working conditions

If working conditions are bad, people find it hard to keep production to a high level. What constitutes bad working conditions depends on the individual and the job involved. Frequently, the worst working conditions look very pleasant but do not offer enough quiet or space (consider the open plan office). As a result of such working conditions, the individual is easily distracted and frustrated; demotivation follows. Move those concerned to perfect working conditions and the production level will return to normal; it will not rise above the norm in proportion to the working conditions' superiority.

Status

People who feel that their status has been downgraded or ignored are unhappy people. Consider the individual who has regularly reported to someone further up the hierarchy and is now told that they must report through an individual at a lower level. At once the status arena is changed and the individual concerned is demoted in his own eyes. Status is important in achieving self-respect.

Company policies and administration

You only need to telephone the inefficient switchboard to know how company policies and administration can cause total frustration. You have probably seen efficient workers reduced to gibbering wrecks by company policy that seems determined to thwart their every effort. That most irritating phrase 'It's more than my job's worth' is a symptom of the worst thought-out company policies. Yet those working for perfect organisations who never frustrate their staff and provide supportive and efficient company administration departments do not report daily thanks from an ever-grateful team.

Supervision

If the supervision is of the type that takes over, the individual gives up and lets the supervisor take on the job - upwards delegation. If it is of the kind that is noticeable only by its lack. The individual will also upwardly delegate the part of the job he cannot finish. Either way, poor supervision is responsible for demotivation, but the perfect, caring, supportive supervisor receives no thanks and is taken for granted.

Inter-personal relations

It is always the little things that cause the greatest problems. Personal habits or small irritating phrases often repeated are the 'stuff' of demotivation. It causes muttering and mumbling and time taken discussing the problem rather than time spent getting on with the job. Yet when all things are perfect, no one says anything because no one notices.

In the demotivators, you are looking at problems that can cause poor performance; faults that must be corrected to improve performance, but areas that once corrected cannot be further improved in order to stimulate performance. In short, the demotivators demotivate when they are wrong, but they do not actively motivate at any time. Put them right and the source of demotivation will be removed. Put them more than right and they may even begin to demotivate all over again.

Motivation factors

The motivators are a different thing altogether. Noticeably, they all centre around the job itself. Some common factors are:

- achievement;
- recognition;
- advancement;
- pleasure in work itself;
- possibility of personal growth;
- responsibility.

Achievement

The achievement of one task motivates the achiever to go on and perform further tasks. Failure to achieve demotivates and may result in frustration and the kind of internal conflict that says 'It's all impossible, I shall cease to try.'

Thus, the lesson is to set achievable targets and make them more rather than fewer, so that they can be achieved and can in their turn motivate the individual to go on achieving more.

Recognition

Achieving a task is part of motivation, but being seen to achieve that task and being rewarded with thanks for the achievement is the final icing on the cake. The phrase 'thank you' often seems to be under-deployed in business life, and yet it immediately reaps disproportionally high rewards. Try using it. Try thanking people for the efforts they make, even if those efforts fail to achieve target. What you'll ensure is that they continue to make the effort and the next time the individual tries he may even achieve the target too.

A task achieved without thanks is a demotivating situation. It may even cause the individual to say 'If that is all the thanks I get, I'll stop trying in future.'

Advancement
Progression up the hierarchy is a form of recognition of achievement and as such motivates the promoted individual. Failure to achieve expected advancement demotivates. It is essential when promoting to remember to speak personally to the individuals who may feel they have been overlooked in the promotion stakes. It will be particularly important if you feel that there is something better on the horizon just waiting for them. If you ignore the overlooked, they will respond by ignoring the organisation.

Pleasure in work itself
The job is capable of giving the most positive and effective rewards of all. Satisfaction in a job well done is available to all. Never under-estimate the motivational powers of knowing how to do a job well and doing that job well. This is the reason why training is so motivational. People who can see new ways to improve the job they do feel good about doing it. The more you train people, the more opportunities you give them to master the job they do, and the greater the resultant motivation.

Personal growth
If asked the question 'Where would you like to be in five years' time?', no one would answer 'In the same position as I am today, making the same mistakes.' Some might well answer that they were satisfied with their lot and quite happy to be doing the same job, but all would say that they would rather not repeat any mistakes and that they would prefer to conquer any problems that may have arisen. Give them no opportunity to develop their talents by training and you will employ demotivated people.

Responsibility
Not everyone wants to be Managing Director, but each individual prefers to be responsible for his own decisions and life. If members

of the team have individual responsibilities, they will work to their best within that team; take away any responsibility and they will have an opportunity to blame someone else for everything that happens.

To motivate people, you need to provide the stimulants of motivation. When they are not present, or are present in negative form, they add to demotivation.

Golden rules for motivation

A simple checklist for motivation is:

- Recognise achievement; thank people when they do things well. Be aware of the efforts they make to achieve on behalf of the organisation.
- Train people so that they can gain the greatest possible pleasure in the job well done and so that they can develop as individuals. Never be afraid to see the individual develop; it will not be at the cost of the organisation, rather to its enrichment.
- Give people responsibility for their own lives and every possible aspect of the job they do. Train them to make the best use of that responsibility.
- Encourage your staff to delegate. Make sure that all resultant delegation is done effectively, passing on the right amount of authority and power, but retaining overall responsibility for the tasks delegated with the delegator while setting up a new line of responsibility from the delegatee to the delegator.
- Pay the fair salary for the job. Make sure people are aware that the salary is fair.
- Never allow grapevine rumours to spread and threaten the stability of jobs.
- Do your best to ensure that the working conditions are the best possible and that company policy and administration react to the workforce and the organisation's development, rather than thwarting it. Never be afraid to change policies that are causing problems.
- Ensure that supervision is concerned, interested and at arm's length. Do not allow people to take over the tasks of others. Give training in how to delegate and how to supervise.

- Resolve conflicts as they arise; never let them fester into demotivating situations.
- Never interfere in people's personal lives, but make sure that they can receive the right level of counselling when they need it. Be tolerant, as an organisation, of the personal problems that arise from time to time and make sure that company policy allows staff time to come to terms with such problems.

Chapter 10
Understanding People

Introduction

Management is about working with people. Modern management is about using the talents of those people in such a way as to ensure that the organisation, the individual and the team all benefit. To motivate a group of people effectively, you need a certain amount of information:

- Why do people do the things they do?
- What makes them feel good?

Some of the answers to why people behave in certain ways lie in transactional analysis (see Chapter 14), which means they are triggered to act by their own patterns of behaviour. Yet still some people seem to remain unmotivated when even your very best efforts at clear transactions are made. The solution to the problem lies in understanding need theory.

Need theory is a collection of theories interpreted by various management writers that show why people seem to seek particular outcomes and why they do not all respond equally to external triggers. Need theory encompasses the work of:

- Maslow: Hierarchy of needs;
- Alderfer: ERG theory;
- Murray: The theory of manifest needs.

Needs hierarchy model

The needs hierarchy model consists of two basic premises. First, people are seen as being motivated by a desire to simultaneously satisfy several types of specific needs. Second, it is suggested that these needs are arranged in a hierarchical form and that people work their way through this hierarchy as their needs are satisfied.

Maslow argues that there are two basic kinds of needs: deficiency needs and growth needs:

- *Deficiency needs:* Needs for safety, belonging, love and respect. These are needs that must be satisfied if the individual is to be healthy and secure. To the extent that these needs are not met, the individual will fail to develop a healthy personality.
- *Growth needs:* Needs for autonomy, self-development, self-realisation, productiveness and self-actualisation. These are needs that relate to the development and achievement of the full individual potential.

People are motivated by five general needs arranged in a hierarchy.

Deficiency needs
- *Level 1 - Physiological:* Basic human needs for food, drink, air, warmth, sleep, shelter, sex, excretion.

In employment terms, these needs are likely to be reflected in the desire for employment. Employment (or unemployment benefit) means enough money to satisfy these first and relatively urgent needs. They are, however, comparatively easily satisfied and the individual quickly passes on to the next level.

- *Level 2 - Safety:* Protection from danger, threat, deprivation; the need for security.

A job is one thing, but what the individual now needs is a permanent job, or at least one that will give him the security of envisaged employment for a reasonable period of time. Thus, the issuing of a contract of employment, the statement of the terms and conditions of the job, and information about the organisation will help to satisfy the employee's security-based needs. Confidence in the employing organisation and its ability to continue to employ him, coupled with an understanding of what he is required to do and the knowledge that he is capable of doing what is required, will fully satisfy his security-based needs.

Thus, in employment terms, this need can be answered by the combination of information, education and training.

- *Level 3 - Belongingness (social):* The need for a sense of belonging, giving and receiving friendship, love, to be accepted by one's peers; the enjoyment of social activities.

In employment terms, this means making the organisation or department something to belong to, giving the individual an environment in which he feels liked and wanted. It may simply mean saying good morning to people when you meet them; it may mean asking questions about their health and hobbies and listening to the reply.

A sense of belonging can be given in many ways. It may mean a uniform or badge - something that identifies the individual with the employing organisation. It may mean a work-based social group offering sport or non-office-based activities. It may be an enhanced sense of teamwork encouraged throughout the organisation. It will be endangered by any threat of change. Change has to be sold very carefully to individuals on this level. It can be fostered by good communications - magazines, presentations, training sessions. It will always be enhanced by recognition of the individual as a human being.

Growth needs

- *Level 4 - Self-esteem:* The need for self-respect and the respect of others. A desire for achievement, acknowledgement, status as appreciation and recognition. A desire for responsibility and autonomy.

Within the organisation, these people tend to seek out the positions of leadership for which they are, of course, admirably suited. People with this need will be well motivated by the delegation of tasks and the handing out of responsibility. In the crudest terms, you might regard them as satisfied in their needs by a larger desk, a better carpet, a private secretary; but those rewards, if used to reflect increased status as a direct result of achievement, are precisely what will indicate the achievement of self-esteem.

It is undoubtedly true that people with this level of need make excellent managers. They are able to say 'no', something people at level 3 often find far harder to do. They are also likely to be capable of judgement to a very high degree. Responding well to training, they are often the people within the organisation most able to adapt to the introduction of knowledge; but also most capable of thwarting change through understanding and knowledge where they feel mistakes are being made.

- *Level 5 - Self-realisation:* The highest need category is the need for self-fulfilment. Here, the individual is concerned with developing his full potential as an individual and of becoming all that it is possible for him to become.

Within an organisation, people in this category can have a very disruptive effect. They are ideas men rather than doers; being creative rather than systematic in their approach, they can disrupt the best laid systems of any organisation. People like this do not tolerate fools gladly and can be very dismissive of their fellow human beings. They will often upset those around them, with no idea that they have had such an effect. Sometimes they are seen as perfectionists in as much as they are seeking the ultimate in achievement; nothing they do is good enough for their own standards.

They are best motivated by being given the kind of role they undertake naturally; creative, innovative, with good back-up from tolerant staff. Many people with this driving force end up running their own organisations or achieving the most senior post within a partnership or conglomerate. On the way up, they are best motivated by training and freedom to develop ideas. You will find most good trainers themselves fall into this category, as often do the technical research people within an organisation.

Movement up the hierarchy
Individuals move up the hierarchy by a process of deprivation and gratification:

- *Deprivation:* When a particular need is unfulfilled, this need will emerge to dominate the individual's consciousness.
- *Gratification:* Once a need is gratified, that need submerges in importance and the next need up the hierarchy is activated.
- *Self-actualisaton:* Unlike the other needs, gratification of the self-actualisation need tends to cause an increase in the potency of the need, instead of a decline.

Growth needs are not easily defined, but the characteristics shown by individuals experiencing these needs include:

- superior perception of reality;
- increased acceptance of self, of others and of nature;
- increased spontaneity;
- increase in problem-centring;
- increased detachment and desire for privacy;
- increased autonomy and resistance to enculturation;
- greater freshness of appreciation and richness of emotional reaction;
- higher frequency of peak experiences;

- increased identification with the human race;
- changed (improved) inter-personal relations;
- more democratic character structure;
- greatly increased creativeness;
- certain changes in the value system.

In most organisations, the majority of employees (some 65 to 75 per cent) will show belongingness/social needs, whereas some 20 to 30 per cent will show growth needs, the bulk of whom will have esteem rather than self-actualisation needs. The remaining few will show safety needs and be the hardest of all to motivate.

Maslow also saw the individual as having two possible further needs that transcend the hierarchy:

- *Cognitive needs:* The desire to know and understand one's environment.
- *Aesthetic needs:* The desire for beauty, harmony and order in nature.

Cognitive needs emphasise the desire of individuals to understand the context of the tasks they perform; aesthetic needs the desire to accept the morality of the organisation.

ERG theory

For Maslow, people travelled upwards through a triangle one step at a time; they achieved a level and remained with that level both in private life and in business life. Alderfer has compacted the triangle into three levels only, but reflects that individuals may have very different needs according to their environment. Not only does he see the satisfaction-progression process, but also one of frustration-regression:

- *Frustration-regression:* When an individual is continually frustrated in his attempts to satisfy growth needs, relatedness needs will re-emerge as the primary motivating force and the individual will redirect his efforts to the lower need levels.

Further, Alderfer suggests that the individual may concentrate on more than one need at a time: he may be a different person at home from the one presented in the office.

Alderfer's theory is based on existence, relatedness and growth, hence ERG.

- *Level 1 - Existence:* Those needs required to sustain human existence, including both the physiological and safety needs described by Maslow.

Where there is employment, there is income; where there is income, there is a chance to satisfy the existence needs. Thus, the employment contract, and the employment environment described at levels 1 and 2 of Maslow, apply identically here.

Now, however, you may see someone regressing to an existence need. This is most likely to be witnessed when individuals are trying to buy or sell a house or are perhaps temporarily homeless due to relocation. If those needs arise, it is most definitely in the interests of the organisation to recognise their existence and do all within its power to satisfy them. This may be going as far as to make relocation allowances or simply to allow time free to deal with a housing problem. Either way, the best solution for the organisation is to give the individual time to satisfy his urgent need, because, until that need is satisfied, concentration at the office will be greatly reduced, as will performance.

- *Level 2 - Relatedness:* Those needs concerning how people relate to their surrounding social environment, including the need for meaningful social and inter-personal relations.

This directly aligns with Maslow's level 3, and once again you are looking at the need for belonging and love. In the centre of the family, the most dismissive self-realisation individual may become someone whose needs are those of relatedness. Once again, you have to recognise that this is the most common area of need; but here too you see that the individual may have this need as an underlying home base need, while in the office his needs are very different.

- *Level 3 - Growth:* Those needs relating to the development of human potential, including the needs of self-esteem and self-actualisation.

Combining the two Maslow levels disguises the very different effects a self-esteem leader and a self-actualisation leader may achieve by concentrating on the growth element.

Manifest needs theory

As with Maslow's theory, Murray felt that individuals could be classified according to the strengths of various needs; or in technical jargon a 'recurrent concern for a goal state'. He believed each need to have two components: a qualitative or directional component, which includes the object towards which the need is directed, and a quantitative or energetic component, which consists of the strength or intensity of the need towards the object.

Murray saw the 13 needs he identified as learned, rather than inherited, and activated by cues from the environment. Thus, an individual might have a need but only pursue the need when the environmental conditions were appropriate, and so the need becomes *manifest*. These needs are as follows:

- *Achievement:* The aspiration to accomplish difficult tasks and to maintain high standards. A willingness to work towards distant goals and to put forward effort to obtain excellence. Any individual experiencing this need responds positively to competition.
- *Affiliation:* An enjoyment of being with friends and people in general coupled with a willingness to make friends easily and to make the effort to do so.
- *Aggression:* An enjoyment of combat and argument. Such an individual may be willing to hurt people who get in the way and seek to get even with people he considers to have done him harm.
- *Autonomy:* A desire for freedom from constraints or restrictions of any kind. Such an individual may be rebellious when faced with restraints.
- *Endurance:* A tenacity and perseverance even in the face of very great difficulties. This individual will not give up easily. Someone who has great patience.
- *Exhibition:* A desire to be the centre of attraction. An individual who seeks an audience.
- *Harm avoidance:* Fear of bodily harm coupled with the avoidance of exciting activities.
- *Impulsiveness:* A tendency to act on the spur of the moment without great thought. This individual may be volatile in emotional expression.
- *Caring:* A sympathetic comforter who is concerned for others.

- *Order:* A dislike of clutter and confusion coupled with a genuine desire for order.
- *Power:* A desire for control and influence. A spontaneous leader.
- *Succourance:* A seeker of sympathy, love and advice. An insecure individual who readily confides in others.
- *Understanding:* A seeker of knowledge, capable of logical thought.

While the manifest needs model encompasses an entire set of needs, most research in organisational settings has focused on the needs of:

- achievement;
- affiliation;
- autonomy;
- power.

These four needs are particularly important for understanding people at work.

Achievement
Achievement motivation training consists of four steps:

- Teach participants how to think, talk and act like a person with high need achievement.
- Stimulate participants to set higher, but carefully planned and realistic work goals for themselves.
- Give the participants knowledge about themselves.
- Create a group sense of belonging from learning about each other's hopes and fears, successes and failures, and from going through an emotional experience together.

Affiliation
The need for human companionship and reassurance. Individuals with a high affiliation need have:

- a strong desire for approval;
- a tendency to conform to the wishes and norms of others when pressurised by people whose friendship they value;
- a sincere interest in the feelings of others.

Autonomy

Individuals with a high need for autonomy prefer situations where they:

- work alone;
- control their own work pace;
- are not hampered by excessive rules and procedures governing their work behaviour.

Power

Need for power represents a desire to influence others and to control one's own environment. The high-power employee will try to control those around him. Employees with high power needs tend to:

- be superior performers;
- have above average attendance records;
- be in supervisory positions.

Personal power

Personal conquest is very important to these individuals; they tend to reject institutional responsibilities. They want their subordinates to be responsible to them and not to the organisation.

Institutional power

These individuals are:

- organisation minded and feel personal responsibility for building up the organisation;
- people who enjoy work and getting things done in an orderly fashion;
- quite willing to sacrifice some of their own self-interest for the welfare of the organisation;
- endowed with a strong sense of justice or equity;
- more mature, ie less defensive and more willing to seek expert advice.

Chapter 11
Difficult People

Dealing with the difficult

Difficult people are different problems according to the situation in which they arise. To deal with them effectively, you need to consider the various situations that are likely to produce difficult people:

- *Selling or persuading:* People who are seeking to buy something from the organisation are often frustrated and angry when they embark on the exercise. The problems they and the inarticulate and indecisive cause need particular handling.
- *Presenting or talking:* The audience at a presentation can contain some very difficult characters indeed.
- *Recruiting or interviewing;* Handling the garrulous or silent types needs particular techniques.
- *The problem employee:* Particularly difficult are those who are poor performers or problem employees who need extra help and guidance to make their full contribution to the organisation.

Selling to or persuading the difficult

The majority of customers are polite, friendly and easy to deal with; it is only the occasional one that is difficult. Sometimes he has justification, while other times he is someone who seems to enjoy being difficult.

To deal with the difficult, you need to hold on to the following facts:

- People demonstrate their frustration in many ways; most of the difficult behaviour you hear is a direct result of frustration. They are all nice people underneath.
- Anxiety can have a strange effect on personality. The telephone in particular makes some people anxious.

- Whatever the person says, it is not a personal insult or intended as such. Do not take personal offence.
- One temper lost is bad enough, to lose yours as well will not improve matters.
- Only the facts matter at the end of the day; hold out for the facts.
- Taking a deep breath before you speak or react gives you time to think. Thinking before you speak or react saves a lot of talking time later.

Complainers

Complaints fall into two categories: the just and unjust. Until you know the facts, you will not know which sort of complaint you are dealing with.

The technique
- Take a deep breath.
- Keep your voice up and friendly.
- Listen to what is being said and take notes.
- *Do not* interrupt, let the speaker get it all off his chest.
- Get the speaker's name and phone number.
- Get any order or service number so that the complaint can be checked.
- Sympathise without being disloyal.
- If the company is at fault apologise.
- Never give excuses, they always sound lame.
- If you promise to call back, *do so.*

Never say:

- You are through to the wrong department. (Even if it is true, it won't solve any problems.)
- It's not my fault. (It probably isn't, but just saying so won't help anyone.)
- I didn't handle this. (See above.)
- Will you write in. (He needs a solution now. Just postponing the dreaded hour will not help at all.)
- We are having lots of problems with ... . (It doesn't help your caller, but it does harm the organisation.)
- You're the sixth one today on about that. (See above.)

Never:

- interrupt the complainer, he will only start all over again;

- automatically accept responsibility or liability, as that may not be the case;
- jump to conclusions before gathering all the facts;
- talk down to the complainer, or accuse him of misuse - it may be true, but it will not smooth ruffled feathers;
- lose your temper;
- appeal for sympathy by trying to justify your position - it will sound like a lame excuse.

Aggression

Aggression is a symptom of both anxiety and frustration. It is the by-product of someone who has failed at a task or feels insecure. Do not confuse it with assertion.

The technique
- Take a deep breath.
- Speak calmly and evenly on a middle pitch.
- Keep your temper.
- Do not respond with aggression.
- Ask for the facts and check your understanding of them.
- Say something like 'I'm sorry this is causing you a problem, but I can only help if you let me' (empathetic assertion).
- Encourage the caller to talk out his feelings of aggression. (The longer he goes on talking, the less aggressive he will become.)
- Be assertive and point out politely the consequences of continued aggressive reactions. (I'm sorry, sir, I realise you are most upset, but I really cannot help you unless you can let me have the total facts without any judgement attached to them.)
- If you cannot calm the telephone caller, arrange to ring back at an agreed time and *do so.*

Vagueness

Talking to a vague customer is very difficult. He will go on for a long time and say very little. You must be patient at all times and try to steer him back to the point.

The technique
- Maintain your patience.
- Write down all the facts as you hear them.
- Use the facts to guide the caller back to the point from time to time.

- Keep a smile in your voice.
- Be businesslike.
- Don't allow the caller to drag you down red herring-strewn byways.
- Keep to the point yourself.
- Keep your temper.
- Don't be abrupt.
- Summarise regularly and particularly at the end of the call.

Unfriendliness

Some individuals are not particularly fond of people in general. They are not likely to be very friendly when using the telephone. Other people confuse being businesslike with unfriendliness. An apparent unfriendly attitude may be a symptom of anxiety or frustration. Either way, do not take it personally; it is not intended personally.

The technique

- Smile as you speak.
- Take nothing personally.
- Keep your voice up and pleasant.
- Deal with the caller as quickly as possible.
- Don't make personal remarks.
- Get the facts and stick to them.
- Don't say 'Thank you for calling' in a pointed manner; your frustration will be wasted energy and have no effect at all.
- Once the call is over and the matter dealt with, forget the caller.

Presenting to or talking to the difficult

Once you open a presentation to questions, you have to deal with the audience as individuals. You, the presenter, become more vulnerable to their attitudes and ideas. Knowing why the individual acts in a certain way will help you to deal with the questions effectively, as shown by the following:

Over-talkative

Why?   May be an eager beaver, a show-off, exceptionally well informed or just naturally wordy.

| What
to do | Ricochet questions back. Interrupt with 'What do the rest of the group think?' Let the group keep him under control. |

Highly argumentative

| Why? | May be aggressive personality, professional heckler or someone who is normally good natured and suffering from stress. |
| What
to do | Keep your temper. Try to find merit in one of his points. Let the group deal with any obvious misstatements. Try to win his co-operation in any recess. |

Helpful

| Why? | Really tries to help, but often ends up being difficult, as he keeps others out of the discussion. |
| What
to do | Cut across him tactfully, by inviting the opinions of others. Thank him and say 'Now let's hear from anyone else with a query.' Let him summarise on your behalf. |

Rambler

| Why? | Insecure and unsure of the point he wants to make he will wander round the topic. He may also like the sound of his own voice. |
| What
to do | Wait till he stops for breath and bring in someone else. Smile, agree that his point is interesting but make it clear it is off the subject. Let the group deal with him. |

Obstinate

| Why? | A prejudiced individual with an axe to grind. Perhaps he has been thwarted by the organisation and is frustrated and demotivated as a result. |
| What
to do | Open his point to the group, let them deal with him. Tell him time is short and you'll be pleased to talk again on the subject on a one-to-one basis later. |

Wrong subject talker

| Why? | He may have entirely missed the point. Perhaps less intelligent than the rest, or a sign that you have used too much jargon. |
| What
to do | I'm sorry, I seem to have misled you; what we need to consider is ... .' |

Complainer

| Why? | Perhaps he has a legitimate complaint. A sign that he |

has been frustrated in achieving his own objectives. Or a professional moaner.

What to do — Let someone else in the group take up his point. Point out that you understand his point of view but are powerless to deal with it at your presentation. Turn it to your advantage to illustrate why your idea will be better.

Inarticulate

Why? — Nervous, less well educated than the rest. Perhaps a junior member of the audience.

What to do — Never say 'What you mean is ... .' Say instead 'Let me put that another way ... .' Try to twist his ideas as little as possible, but turn them into sense.

Definitely wrong

Why? — Has not been listening, perhaps prejudiced or ill informed.

What to do — 'Well, that is one way of looking at it ... .' 'I see your point, but how can we reconcile it to ... .' Don't squash him or let the rest of the audience do so.

Opinion seeker

Why? — Could be looking for advice or trying to catch you out. Either insecure, a genuine seeker of knowledge or a know-all.

What to do — Try never to take sides or the responsibility for someone else's problems. Restate your view and emphasise that it is just that. Use him to introduce your summary.

Silent minority

Why? — Bored, shy, insecure, indifferent, feels too superior, all are possible.

What to do — Try to arouse his interest. Draw out others in the audience near him. Ask him a provocative question. Ignore him, you don't need to court problems unless he is someone very important to your presentation.

What to do when difficult people get together

Personality clashes

- Emphasise points of agreement and minimise points of disagreement.

- Draw their attention to the purpose of the presentation.
- Bring in someone else.
- Ask them to put their differences aside for a moment.

Side conversation
- Ask one of the individuals a question.
- Restate the last remark and ask one of the talkers his opinion.
- Carry on and ignore them if you can.
- Try not to embarrass them; let the group tell them to shut up.

Recruiting or interviewing the difficult

Not all the candidates you interview will be possible employees. However good your preselection system, some mistakes or problems will present themselves for interview at your request. Not all of your interview problems will be insoluble, however.

The common types of problem encountered are as follows:

- The candidate is unsuitable; this becomes apparent very early on.
- It is difficult to understand the candidate.
- The candidate is boring.
- The candidate is shy and obviously nervous.
- The candidate is garrulous.

The unsuitable candidate
The temptation to make an early judgement, possibly based only on the candidate's appearance, should be avoided. On the other hand, waste as little time as possible interviewing a candidate to whom you have no intention of offering a job.

If you are going to cut an interview short, having made the decision that the candidate is totally unsuitable, be very sure of your judgement. Many people do create a bad impression in the early stages of an interview, very often through nervousness.

Only the interviewer can devise a total list of undesirable characteristics that would bring an interview to a rapid close. Be prepared to defend them, however, under employment legislation. Such a list might include answers to questions that indicate:

- a drinking or drugs problem;
- a dishonest trait;
- total physical unsuitability.

If the candidate really is totally unsuitable, and you are satisfied that your judgement is accurate and fair, you must then consider the potential effect on your organisation of an abrupt end to the interview.

With any individual applicant, you always need to be aware of the image of the organisation that he will carry away with him. Even abbreviated interviews can end on a pleasant note; make sure yours do.

Cutting the interview short

The mechanics of cutting an interview short can be difficult. If you have planned to use a second interviewer, bring that interview forward - you will need an early warning system for this. If you have not planned for a second interviewer to be involved, but have potential understudies available, contact one and let him conduct part of the interview. Again, you will need an early warning system, and to say to the candidate 'I should particularly like Mr X to meet you.'

Getting another person involved allows you a chance to think your tactics out carefully and enables you to reconsider your judgement. It also gives you a valuable second opinion.

If you are really on your own then:

- continue to the bitter end;
- cut the interview short, telling the candidate that you will not be able to consider him for the job, giving him a good reason;
- shorten the interview by eliminating elements as you go along.

Language problems

If the candidate is difficult to understand, assuming that you speak good English and are not deaf!, it is likely to be for reasons of:

- accent;
- speech defect;
- unfamiliarity with the English language.

The first two reasons are unlikely to change over a short period. If such a problem would genuinely affect the work of the candidate, you will need to reject him. If the problem would hardly affect the work to be done by the candidate, draw attention to the problem and discuss how it can be overcome. Remember that interview nerves can make a stutter or an accent far worse than it really is.

If the candidate is unfamiliar with the English language you must decide:

- Does it matter?
- Does he have other attributes that outweigh the language problem?
- Are you prepared to pay for language tuition?

The boring candidate

- Some people are more boring than others.
- It is easier to be bored some times of the day than others.
- The average human has a concentration span of 45 minutes.

All these factors mean that sooner or later you will meet a candidate who bores you.

- Try not to show it.
- If you are desperate to yawn, get up and walk around.
- Do not conduct interviews after heavy lunches.
- Change the subject.
- Ask yourself what effect the candidate will have within the organisation.

The shy or nervous candidate

Most interviewers are nervous too. In fact, if neither party suffered from nerves it would probably be a very boring interview; no one would have the adrenalin needed to lift the discussion.

- Try to relate to the candidate.
- Talk about yourself.
- Let the candidate see you are aware he is nervous and want to help.
- Give the candidate time to relax.
- Give the candidate your whole attention.
- If shyness is acute, discuss it and its potential effect on the job.

The garrulous candidate

Very often a garrulous candidate is only displaying his version of nerves. Try to be sympathetic, if you suspect this to be the case.

Never be afraid to interrupt and redirect the flow of what he is saying in mid-stream; the truly garrulous will be used to this happening.

Draw attention to his garrulousness and ask questions such as:

- Can you work quietly?
- Do you like to work alone?

Remember, in a populated office, the truly garrulous person will hold up work and may cause others to complain. Working alone he may wander off to find someone to talk to.

The problem employee

The problem employee is someone whose behaviour does not match the norm expected for the organisation. Such employees are likely to offer three types of performance problem:

- Job performance problems.
- Inter-personal problems with other members of staff.
- Behavioural problems.

Some employees will suffer from all three types of problem, while others will be less complicated, showing the symptoms of only one or two of the problems.

Job performance problems
Quite simply, the employee concerned cannot or will not perform the job to a standard acceptable within the organisation.

Cannot perform to an acceptable standard
When the employee cannot perform to an acceptable standard, there are two possible reasons: either he needs additional training to be able to undertake the task effectively or he is incapable of understanding the task and the training already given. The solution is simple: on the one hand give the extra training, making sure that every possible encouragement and training aid is used (see Chapter 8); on the other hand, transfer the individual to a simpler job or cease to employ him.

Will not perform to an acceptable standard
When the problem is a motivational one, it will possibly be harder to solve. The time element is all important here.

Recently experienced demotivational feelings can often be cured at the initial moment of experience. Being passed over for promotion is a good example. If, when you promoted the alternative individual, you failed to speak to each member of staff who might have expectations for the post, it is likely that you will have demotivated some. Now you have spotted that demotivation, you must speak to them and discuss how they can be more successful next time around in the promotion stakes.

Those who have been nurturing a grudge against supervision methods for a period of time will not simply recover with a chat. Action is needed, either to improve the supervision methods or perhaps to part company with the demotivated employee. Always realise that demotivation breeds demotivation and if one employee becomes demotivated, and as a result a poor performer, it is quite likely that others will do so too. The problem must be dealt with before it reaches epidemic proportions (see Chapter 9 for motivational techniques).

Inter-personal problems with other members of staff

One employee fails to get on with another. In its simplest form, the problem may not affect performance, but be a regular irritation to the work group. Even at this low level it will affect team performance. It does not matter what the problem is, the first step to solution is to talk to the employee producing the unacceptable behaviour and point out the problems he is causing. If you have an atmosphere of teamwork, realisation of the strain put on the team may be enough to solve the problem. If that doesn't work, you will probably need to run a counselling session.

Behavioural problems

Problem behaviour can be as minor as unacceptable dress for work and as major as drug or alcohol dependency. First, identify your problem and then look to see what its underlying causes are. Often the problem is likely to be a method of drawing attention to the individual concerned; the need is to find out what causes the cry for attention.

Before going any further, it must be stressed that dealing with behavioural problems of a serious nature is not for the willing but untrained manager. The untrained can take counselling to a certain stage, but must realise they will have to hand over to the professionals, should the problem prove to be of greater magnitude.

The external causes behind the problem may be as a result of:

- cultural background;
- work environment;

- lack of resources;
- sex role stereotyping;
- available training;
- the generation gap.

Cultural background

You live in a multi-cultural society. Gone are the days when it was possible to dictate certain cultural behavioural patterns. Now, you need to be flexible, to be prepared to respect the cultural preferences of other groups. Give people a chance to respond to their own backgrounds, discuss any problems openly and the work society will become harmonious again.

Work environment

You might be dealing with problems as simple as the lack of light or heat for an employee who is sensitive to such things. The working environment cannot be perfect. If you get it as near to perfect as it can be, and are flexible in the process, you eliminate another form of problem.

The psychological work environment is yet another form of problem. Supervision needs to be right for the individual and to vary with the individuals in the organisation. Once again, you need to be flexible, but above all else, to train supervisors well (see Chapter 7).

Lack of resources

If the resources are not there to support the effort, even the most efficient begin to tire of the struggle. Working on outdated machinery which leads to breakdowns requiring frequent maintenance and mistakes by the operator is not conducive to effective performance. The answer is to upgrade the technology as soon as possible.

Instant upgrading is not always possible, particularly in the smaller organisation. Where this is the case, take the time to discuss the problem with the team and tell them how soon you may be able to schedule the new equipment into the profit plan. Give the team a chance to interject their suggestions. If they feel you are trying to do something about the problem, the demotivation factors may be removed.

Sex role stereotyping

This problem does not only affect women, but it does cause a great deal of frustration to them. Certain businesses are orientated towards one sex and as such seem to produce patterns of behaviour to exclude the opposite sex. Engineering, for example, is still predominantly a male-orientated profession; women engineers often have to put up with unacceptable behaviour patterns from their male colleagues while trying to make their way within the profession.

The assumption that the male is the boss and the female the subordinate is frequently wrong nowadays, but it is still made, much to the annoyance of both parties.

The cure to the problem is awareness. Ask employees how they feel about certain behaviour and make changes where necessary. Raise employees' consciousness of sex role issues. Lead by example, but don't let the issue take over an otherwise effective organisation.

Available training

People's skills become out of date very quickly nowadays. Be aware of the problem and regard it as part of the obligations of the organisation to keep employee skills up to date. Such a policy will not only affect employee behaviour, but it will enhance the organisation's profitability too.

Once again, you need to lead by example. Embrace change as the way forward into the future, not something to be thwarted and hindered, and only finally suffered under duress.

The generation gap

The real gap is not one of age, but of values. The only way to handle it is to get either side of the gap and understand the values of both parties. Each party can learn from the other, but the learning needs to be controlled discussion aimed at getting the best from the system of values available.

The internal causes behind behavioural problems may be due to:

- personality factors;
- personal habits;
- inadequate skills;
- learning potential;
- low motivation;
- maturity.

Personality factors

If the performance relies on teamwork, you must take into account the personality factors. They are really the manifest needs described in Chapter 10 and, as such, you need to take care in the mix of personalities who work together. There is little reason in appointing a leader who is shy and tries to keep a low profile to lead an aggressive group. The leadership will fail and the group underperform.

The solution is to know your employees, recruit others to fit in with the workforce and make sure you mix the teams effectively.

Personal habits

Nowadays, the biggest problem is that of the smoker, who is likely to be isolated within organisations. Other problems may include less obvious behavioural patterns, perhaps excessive cleanliness or slovenliness, which after a while can drive co-workers to distraction.

You cannot ignore the problem because it is a personal one. A policy on smoking or not smoking is probably a wise thing to establish within the modern working environment. Consider new employees accordingly.

Most problems of this nature can be dealt with by separating the individuals concerned or by counselling. Telling someone they smell is not a pleasant job, but a necessary one for the survival of the organisation.

Inadequate skills

Many firms employ staff at higher levels without testing their skills. They take on managers and other professionals without any kind of skills test, relying on the qualification alone or perhaps on the information given by the employee himself. Nor can you rely on references to tell you that the employee is capable of doing the job.

The answer lies first in the selection process. This must be designed to ensure that all employees are subjected to skills testing, even if it is only a discussion of likely problem situations and how they might treat them. Consider also the possibility of in-tray exercises.

The second level of the answer lies in recognition of the need to provide adequate updating training for all employees.

Learning potential

The assumption that the job will remain the same throughout the life of the organisation is a false one. For this reason, it is necessary to be convinced of the employee's learning potential at the time of recruitment. Once employed, an individual should be alive to the learning opportunities and set an environment that rewards self-development.

Low motivation

The causes of low motivation must be discovered. See Chapter 9 for details.

Maturity

Maturity is not always a function of age. In general terms, however, it is fair to assume that the greater the number of experiences through which the individual has come, the greater the resultant maturity. Mature people are self-motivated and prefer to work to their own stimulus. Immature people need greater guidance and a more directive leadership style. Immature people look for role models and it is essential that they are given the right role model: the one that will eventually remove their childish habits and teach them adult ones.

How to counsel the problem employee

Privacy

Not only must the session be run in complete privacy, but there should be secrecy as to its taking place at all. Other employees should not be in a position to speculate on what is going on and why. A private office, an appointed time and agreed involvement are all essential.

Consequences

The purpose of the session is to spell out to the employee the consequences of continuing the present problem behaviour. The employee must then be allowed to make a choice between those consequences and the preferable ones awaiting reformed behaviour. If the employee's choice is to change the behaviour pattern, then you will need to show him how to make the necessary changes. If the choice is not to change, you will need to be aware of very definite consequences. Employment legislation will take a hand here and may involve inviting a witness to the session.

How to Solve Your People Problems

One point at a time
No matter how many items form part of the discussion, take them one at a time systematically. If you just let rip with all your complaints at once, the employee will react with anger or defensiveness or even a sense of futility, none of which will help the situation under review.

Give specific examples
'You're doing a lousy job' tells the employee nothing. 'What went wrong on the XYZ contract, I was expecting great things that didn't happen?' is specific enough to take the personal nature out of the complaint.

Focus on the problem
Don't direct your wrath towards the whole individual, merely direct it justifiably towards the behaviour that is causing the problem. Stick to the facts at all times and refuse to make personal comments.

Mean what you say
If you can't carry out your threats, don't make them.

Know when you are beaten
Counselling may affect your managerial role. Never try to solve the problem, just show the way to the solution.

Never take on personal and private problems
Remember that professonal help should be given as early as possible if it is to be truly effective. Don't delay it by interfering in a problem too great for your powers.

Remember
- Encourage self-awareness.
- Examine the diet of a poor performer.
- Respect his choices.
- Stop enabling any addiction - to work, to drugs, to behaviour.
- Suggest outside stimulus to calm on the job performance.
- Make him aware of professional help.

Finally, do not fall into the following traps:
- The poor performer who is not a poor performer, just someone whose habits and attitudes you do not like.

- Getting even with someone for something they did to you or something/someone you care about.
- Putting off dealing with problem behaviour because of a personal need to be liked.

Chapter 12
Conflict

Conflict is part of working with people; a natural event that must form part of nearly every working day. As such, conflict need not be a problem, but it can be allowed to become a problem if it is handled ineffectively or allowed to last so long that it begins to destroy the working environment.

Types of conflict

Conflict in the organisation arises for many reasons; four clear types of conflict emerge:

- *Goal conflict:* Where one person or one group desires a different outcome from others.
- *Cognitive conflict:* Where one person or one group holds ideas that are in conflict with those held by others.
- *Affective conflict:* Where one person's or group's emotions, feelings or attitudes are incompatible with others.
- *Behavioural conflict:* Where one person or group behaves in a way that is unacceptable to others.

Goal conflict is perhaps the most dangerous to the organisation as a whole. Groups within the organisation who no longer hold the goals of that organisation as their own may well develop alternative goals at odds with the objectives of the organisation. The introduction of new systems and ideas is frequently met by just this kind of conflict. In fear of the changes that are to come, the group develops goals that are at total odds with the introduction of change and instead try to avert the change from taking place.

Cognitive conflict is the introduction of new ideas and as such the dynamics of change. Cognitive conflict will always be present at the development of new work groups and with the introduction of new members of staff. Indeed, it is one of the reasons for introducing new members of staff, for cognitive conflict is essential if an organisation is to react to the world about it and develop new ideas.

Affective conflict involves the individual's emotions and as such is the hardest to control. People in affective conflict are never reasonable and often the outsider cannot see any reason why the conflict should exist at all. Strong political and ethnic attitudes and beliefs come into this category. There is often very little that can be done effectively to solve this type of conflict, beyond the drastic removal of one of the warring parties.

Behavioural conflict is frequently resolved within the group itself. People who wish to remain members of the group usually conform to its acccepted patterns of behaviour, even where they themselves do not fully agree with the patterns. Deep-set behavioural conflict often results in a member leaving the group in search of a more suitable one.

Each type of conflict can appear on four levels:

- *Intra-personal* - conflict within one person.
- *Inter-personal* - conflict between two individuals.
- *Intra-group* - conflict within one group.
- *Inter-group* - conflict between groups.

Intra-personal cognitive conflict is the stuff of which geniuses are made - the inner conflict that chases new ideas while striving for the slow development of perfection within the old. As such, it can be extremely painful to the sufferer and result in outbreaks of apparently unpredictable behaviour. If you seek new ideas, inventions and change within the organisation, there is a need for intra-personal conflict sufferers and the problems their behaviour brings. There is even an argument that says they should not be helped to solve this conflict, since its ending will also be likely to end the creative phase of their development.

All other intra-personal conflicts cause poor performance by the individual concerned and must be dealt with if the output is to be at an acceptable level.

Inter-personal conflict is perhaps the most unpleasant to work with. If the individuals meet every day and carry on a war between themselves, it is unsettling for the entire department. Such conflict can only be tolerated where it produces new ideas. Thus, once again, it is the cognitive conflict that works in favour of the organisation. All other inter-personal conflicts destroy and must themselves be stopped as soon as possible.

Intra-group conflict is the normal development of working groups. Termed 'storming' in the group jargon (see page 71), it is the process through which every group passes whenever a new member joins. It can take any conflict form, although as ever the most productive form will be cognitive. Prolonged storming within a group, however, is not acceptable, since it reduces morale and may well become the acceptable pattern of behaviour for the group, replacing the performance criteria set by the organisation.

Inter-group conflict is often encouraged by the organisation. Comparison levels between groups stress competition, and competition can lead to a great striving for excellence. While the inter-group conflict does not detract the warring factions from the ultimate organisation goal, it is a worthwhile part of organisation life. As soon as it begins to interfere with that goal, it must be stopped and the energies redirected.

Development of conflict

Whatever the type, whomsoever the conflict affects, it always arises out of a four-stage process as follows.

Frustration
Conflict situations originate where an individual or group feels frustrated or about to be frustrated in pursuit of important goals. The causes can be:

- performance goals;
- promotion;
- pay rises;
- power;
- scarce economic resources;
- rules;
- values;
- in short, anything the individual or group cares about.

Thus, failing to achieve a target or goal may cause the start of the conflict cycle.

Conceptualisation
At the second stage, the parties to the potential conflict attempt:

- to understand the nature of the problem;
- what they themselves want as a resolution;
- the various strategies they may employ to achieve that resolution.

This is the stage where conflict can most often be turned to good use or avoided if careful negotiations are employed. It is the moment of self- or behaviour analysis. Effective analysis will determine the right behaviour pattern for the future to correct the frustration felt as a result of goal failure. False analysis will lead to behaviour that is doomed to increase the frustration.

Behaviour
As a result of the conceptualisation process, parties to the conflict attempt to implement their resolution by behaving in the pattern they have selected as most likely to achieve the desired result.

Instant conceptualisation, when the party to the conflict is still feeling frustrated, usually leads to worse behavioural patterns and further conflict.

Outcome
If the outcome results in one party feeling dissatisfied, the seeds will be sown for further conflict. Whatever the result, the outcome will be part of the patterning and conditioning that set the possible patterns of behaviour in future conflict.

Conflict can become an ever-decreasing circle; the frustration leads to instant and false conceptualisation, which in its turn causes further wrong behaviour, the outcome of which is further frustration and even more false conceptualisation. The only way out of such a situation is to break the conflict at the conceptualisation stage.

Handling conflict

It is only at the conceptualisation stage of conflict development that the most effective solutions can be found, so part of handling conflict must be watching for the process of conflict development to begin.

Once the pattern of the developing conflict has been established, help or self-help can be administered. Beware of starting too early and catching the remaining frustration, which can easily turn to anger. Trying to solve a conflict with an angry person is almost impossible and can result in the permanent rejection of the most sound and sensible idea.

Competing

Competing is handling conflict head on. It is standing firm and rejecting the views and beliefs of the other party or standing between the warring factions and demanding that the war cease. Use it where:

- a quick decision is vital;
- unpopular ideas on important issues must be implemented;
- issues are vital to the organisation and you know you are right;
- opponents take advantage of non-competitive behaviour.

Collaborating

Collaborating is less than the art of total compromise. It will in all probability be the chosen method for dealing with cognitive conflict to ensure that no *one* good idea is needlessly sacrificed to the solution of conflict. To collaborate, take the ideas that come from both parties to the conflict and try to find a way of developing them all, without detracting from the overall goal. Use it where:

- both sets of concerns are too important to be compromised;
- your objective is to learn;
- you wish to merge insights from different people;
- you need commitment;
- you need to dispel feelings that have interfered with a relationship.

Compromising

Compromise is the art of win-win negotiation. Both parties to the conflict should feel that they have won but neither should feel any sense of loss. You will achieve it by using negotiation tactics as described in Chapter 13. Use it where:

- goals are important but not worth the disruption of more assertive behaviour;
- opponents with equal power are committed to mutually exclusive goals;
- you wish to achieve temporary settlements to complex issues;
- time pressure is great;
- you need a back-up to failed collaboration or competition.

Avoiding

Avoiding means deciding not to get involved in the conflict and asking that it be solved elsewhere. Use it where:

- the issue is trivial;
- more important issues are pressing;
- there is no chance of satisfying your concerns;
- the potential disruption outweighs the benefits of resolution;
- people need to cool down;
- gathering information might help;
- others can resolve the conflict more effectively;
- issues seem intangible.

Accommodating
Accommodating is the art of accepting the situation and agreeing to back down in conflict. Use it where:

- you are wrong;
- issues are more important to others than to yourself;
- you can build social credits for future issues;
- you need to minimise loss, as you are outmatched, and losing harmony and stability are especially important;
- subordinates need to learn by mistakes made.

Conflict can be constructive

Don't forget that conflict can be constructive. Without conflict an organisation cannot grow and develop. Conflict is an essential part of change and creativity. Use it for:

- problem solving;
- engendering new ideas;
- personality development;
- training and educating;
- role playing to establish potential problem areas.

Conflict and anxiety

As a result of conflict, individuals often experience considerable anxiety but can find no easy way to reduce it. This is particularly the case where a solution to the conflict seems unobtainable or long term. As a result, the suffering individuals apply defence mechanisms. Three group types of defence mechanism may be employed:

Aggressive defence mechanisms
- *Fixation* - won't budge from a point of view.

How to Solve Your People Problems

- *Displacement* - redirecting pent up emotions towards hate objects or individuals.
- *Negativism* - active or passive resistance, no co-operation.

Compromise defence mechanisms

- *Compensation* - individual works harder to make up for feeling inadequate.
- *Identification* - individual enhances self-esteem by copying the behaviour of someone he admires.
- *Projection* - individual pretends that his own undesirable traits are in fact attributable to others.
- *Rationalisation* - individual justifies behaviour and beliefs by providing explanations for them.
- *Reaction formation* - urges not acceptable to consciousness are repressed and the opposite attitudes displayed in their place by the individual.

Withdrawal defence mechanisms

- *Conversion* - emotional conflicts are expressed in muscular, sensory or bodily symptoms of disability, malfunctioning or pain.
- *Fantasy* - day-dreaming provides an escape from reality.
- *Regression* - individual returns to an earlier and less mature level of adjustment in the face of frustration.
- *Repression* - impulses, experiences and feelings that are psychologically disturbing, because they arouse a sense of guilt or anxiety, are completely excluded from consciousness.
- *Resignation, apathy and boredom* - switching off.
- *Withdrawal or flight* - leaving the area of frustration either physically or mentally.

The anxiety feelings caused by conflict show in the conceptualisation and the eventual behaviour outcome. Part of the resolution of conflict must be the treatment of the anxiety-based reactions. This is particularly important when trying to resolve one's own conflicts. Awareness of the normal reaction to anxiety should help to select the right approach at conceptualisation.

Chapter 13
Negotiation

The art of negotiating

Negotiation is the use of knowledge, time and power to influence the behaviour of other people so that you can achieve your goals. The steps are as follows:

- *Define needs:* What do you and the parties you represent need to get from this negotiation?
- *Check resources:* What resources do you have to help you with the negotiation? Who can you use? What are the facts?
- *Know limitations:* At what stage will you have to hand a negotiation over to someone else? How far is your side prepared to go in conceding to the other side?
- *Understand options:* List the possible options that could come out of the negotiation. How many of them are possible for your side to accept?
- *Formulate goals:* Decide what you hope to achieve and the elements of the goal that cannot be compromised.
- *Prepare for the encounter:* Prepare both mentally and physically.

Preparation

For the other party
- *Recognise the need:* What does he want from the negotiation?
- *Understand and define that need:* How strongly are those needs likely to be felt?
- *Check alternatives:* What possible alternatives are there? Will he have thought of them all?
- *Understand the options:* Realise the areas where your opponent cannot afford to compromise and the options that can remain open for him.
- *Know the power of choice:* Understand that he is able to choose.

127

For yourself

- *Recognise your own need:* What do you hope to prove by this negotiation?
- *Check alternative resources:* Are there alternatives that you have rejected because of your assumptions or attitude?
- *Define options:* Write down your options; keep them all open.
- *Set goals:* Write down your goal and stick to it.
- *Set limits to goals:* How far they can be compromised? Make a careful list of areas that can be compromised.
- *Consider the effect of the passage of time:* Remember, what was important yesterday may change in the light of the negotiation.
- *Consider the time pressures:* Set time criteria.
- *Set cost limits:* What are the costs that are acceptable? Do not go above them.
- *Establish gain to be achieved:* Write down what the anticipated achievements are to be.

Confrontation or collaboration?

The opposite parties in a negotiation are counterparts. Some negotiators think of their counterparts as the enemy. To negotiate, the two parties will have to come together; therefore life is much easier if you think of your counterpart as a friend: *attitude determines outcome.*

Negative orientation: The enemy
- Opposition
- Opposition leads to suspicion
- Suspicion leads to aggression
- Aggression leads to deadlock

The confrontational mindset:
Counterpart = adversary
Difference   = conflict
Resources   = weapons

Positive orientation: The friend
- Opposition
- Opposition leads to co-operation
- Co-operation leads to partnership
- Partnership leads to settlement

The collaborative mindset:
Counterpart = partner
Difference   = opportunities
Resources = incentives to co-operate

How to conduct collaborative negotiation
The collaborative negotiator must show the following character traits if he is to succeed:

- Interest in the needs of the counterpart.
- Understanding of the counterpart's needs.
- Willingness to co-operate and compromise.
- Mind focused on settlement not obstacles.
- Mutual gain = win-win.

As a collaborative negotiator, you will achieve the following gains:

- Difference leads to opportunities.
- Co-operation leads to trust.
- Preparation leads to understanding.
- Counterpart becomes partner.
- Mutual problem solving brings settlement.

The stages of collaborative negotiation are:

- Analyse the needs of the counterpart.
- Demonstrate a desire for co-operation.
- Emphasise mutual interest.
- Demonstrate understanding of counterpart's needs.
- Understand the relationship betwen counterpart's needs and own resources and goals.

Power in negotiation

- Bargaining power is measured relative to that of the counterpart.
- Bargaining power is determined by external economic and political factors.
- It is preferable to negotiate from a powerful position.
- The balance of power in a negotiation is determined by the urgency of each side's needs and assets.

The power of persuasion
- Persuasion gives the negotiator power.

- Persuasion is a personal form of power.
- Persuasion can be learned and improved.
- Persuasion depends on selling ability.
- Persuasion depends on positive tone.
- Persuasion plays both to economic reasoning and to personal factors.

Assessing the balance of power

- How badly do you need what the counterpart has?
- How soon must your needs be fulfilled?
- What are the consequences should your negotiation break down?
- How badly does the counterpart need what you bring to the table?
- What are your counterpart's time restraints?
- Are there alternatives to dealing with this counterpart?
- Who is in the position of most immediate and greatest need?
- Who has the superior position with respect to resources?

How to win

Set sensible expectations

- Set high goals.
- Use realistic assumptions.
- Decide areas open for significant compromise.
- Decide areas not open for compromise.
- Be clear about what you hope to achieve.

Use the right level of authority

- Know your limits.
- Find out the counterpart's limits.
- Don't let someone with limited authority wear you down.
- Try to bypass negotiators with limited authority.
- Share responsibility with those on whose behalf you negotiate.

Go for win-win

- Win-win brings together different needs and creates opportunities for mutual gain.
- Win-lose makes enemies who fight harder next time.
- Focus on the goal.
- Confine disagreement to ideas.
- Avoid personal issues.

Use time with care
- Haste makes waste; the best negotiations take time.
- Be prepared; negotiate before the crisis.
- Over a barrel; urgency may force concessions.
- Sleep on it; avoid marathon sessions.

Use questions
- Ask them even if you know the answers.
- Ask for help.
- Listen.
- Question what is negotiable; don't be thrown by 'company policy'.

Personalise the negotiation
- Form bonds of respect and trust.
- Remember people as well as things are involved.
- Make personal contact, relax, smile.
- Make it matter; show you care.
- Relate to the organisation.

Use time
- Allow time for frequent recesses.
- Move the bargaining at a deliberate pace.
- Use recesses to calm down or research further.
- Maintain self-control at all times.

Watch for unspoken needs
- Remember your counterpart may have a hidden agenda.
- Watch the body language.
- Stay awake.
- Meet your counterpart's needs.
- Remember personal and social needs can often be met at minimum expense.

Finally:
- Aim to control the situation.
- Believe in yourself.
- Keep written records for the future.

Trouble-shooting

The likely needs or wants of your counterpart
- To feel good about himself.
- To avoid further trouble and risk.
- To be recognised as a man of good judgement.
- Knowledge.
- An easy life.
- To be listened to.
- To keep his job.
- Promotion.
- To save time.
- To be liked.
- Power.

How to break an impasse
Sometimes you hit a situation when nothing seems possible. No one is willing to give way. The only way out is change.

- Change:
  — the shape of the package;
  — a member of the team;
  — the time limits on part of the negotiation;
  — the risk mix;
  — the time scale of performance;
  — the bargaining emphasis;
  — the type of contract;
  — the base for a percentage.
- Call a mediator.
- Arrange a summit meeting.
- Add options.
- Set up a joint study committee.
- Tell a joke.

How to make concessions
- Leave yourself room to negotiate.
- Encourage the counterpart to open up first.
- Let the counterpart make the first concession.
- Make him work for his gains.
- Conserve concessions.

- Don't give tit-for-tat concessions.
- A promise is a concession at a discount rate.
- Don't be afraid to say 'no'.
- Keep track of your concessions.
- Retreat from a concession if you have made a mistake.
- Don't give in too much too quickly.

Difficult counterparts

The majority of counterparts are polite and friendly and easy to deal with; it is only the occasional one that is difficult. Sometimes he has justification, while at other times he is someone who seems to enjoy being difficult.

To deal with the difficult, you need to hold on to the following facts:

- People demonstrate their frustration in many ways; most of the difficult behaviour you hear is a direct result of frustration. They are all nice people underneath.
- Anxiety can have a strange effect on personality.
- Whatever the person says, it is not a personal insult or intended as such. Do not take personal offence.
- One temper lost is bad enough, to lose yours as well will not improve matters.
- Only the facts matter at the end of the day; hold out for the facts.
- Taking a deep breath before you speak or react gives you time to think. Thinking before you speak or react saves a lot of talking time later.

Complainers
Complaints fall into two categories: the just and unjust. Until you know the facts, you will not know which sort of complaint you are dealing with.

The technique
- Take a deep breath.
- Keep your voice up and friendly.
- Listen to what is being said and take notes.
- *Do not* interrupt, let the speaker get it all off his chest.
- Check the validity of complaints about the past.
- Sympathise without being disloyal.

- If the company is at fault, apologise.
- Never give excuses, they always sound lame.
- If you promise to do something, *do it.*

Never say:

- I'm not the person to talk to about . . . . (Even if it is true, it won't solve any problems.)
- It's not my fault. (It probably isn't, but just saying so won't help anyone.)
- I didn't handle this. (See above.)
- We are having lots of problems with . . . . (It doesn't help your caller, but it does harm the organisation.)

Never:

- interrupt the complainer, he will only start all over again;
- automatically accept responsibility or liability, as that may not be the case;
- jump to conclusions before gathering all the facts;
- talk down to your complainer, or accuse him of misuse - it may be true, but it will not smooth ruffled feathers;
- lose your temper;
- appeal for sympathy by trying to justify your position - it will sound like a lame excuse.

Aggression

Aggression is a symptom of both anxiety and frustration. It is the by-product of someone who has failed at a task or feels insecure. Do not confuse it with assertion.

The technique

- Take a deep breath.
- Speak calmly and evenly on a middle pitch.
- Keep your temper.
- Do not respond with aggression.
- Ask for the facts and check your undestanding of them.
- Say something like 'I'm sorry this is causing you a problem, but I can only help if you let me' (empathetic assertion).
- Encourage your counterpart to talk out his feelings of aggression. (The longer he goes on talking, the less aggressive he will become.)
- Be assertive and point out politely the consequences of

continued aggressive reactions.
- If you cannot calm your counterpart, arrange a break.

Vagueness
Negotiating with a vague counterpart is very difficult. He will go on for a long time and say very little. You must be patient at all times and try to steer him back to the point.

The technique
- Maintain your patience.
- Write down all the facts as you hear them.
- Use the facts to guide your counterpart back to the point from time to time.
- Keep a smile in your voice.
- Be businesslike.
- Don't allow yourself to be dragged down red herring-strewn byways.
- Keep to the point yourself.
- Keep your temper.
- Don't be abrupt.
- Summarise regularly.

Unfriendly
Some individuals are not particularly fond of people in general. They are not likely to be very friendly when negotiating. Other people confuse being businesslike with unfriendliness. An apparent unfriendly attitude may be a symptom of anxiety or frustration. Either way, do not take it personally; it is not intended personally.

The technique
- Smile as you speak.
- Take nothing personally.
- Keep your voice up and pleasant.
- Deal with the points as quickly as possible.
- Don't make personal remarks.
- Get the facts and stick to them.
- Once the negotiation is over and the matter dealt with, forget your counterpart.

Chapter 14
Communication

The nature of communication

Spotting communication failure is not hard; examples can be seen all around you every day and they constitute some of the major people problems you will encounter:

- Angry people shouting because they cannot be understood.
- Frustrated people sulking because no one listened to them.
- Silent people opting out because they could not understand.
- Bored people staring around them because the communication is on the wrong level.
- Miserable people who took everything personally.
- Chatterboxes talking at each other rather than to each other.
- Firms that have gone into liquidation because they never got their message across.
- Bosses who are frustrated by the activities of the firm's grapevine.
- Poor industrial relations because neither party understands the other.
- Lost orders because no one understood.

The list is endless. Communication failure is one of the greatest management problems in the UK today, mainly because people realise neither the importance of getting it right nor the difficulties in the art of effective communication. Because people were born with the ability to speak, see and hear, they take communication for granted. Take away one of those senses and it becomes a much more thoughful task.

Factors involved in communication

All communication involves:

- a sender;
- an encoder;

- a medium;
- a decoder;
- a receiver.

The sender

The sender is the person who transmits the message - the originator of the phone call or conversation. The sender generates the content of the message and decides to whom it should be sent. Once he has thought out the message, he encodes it.

The encoder

The encoder transforms the message into the appropriate medium. The encoder may simply be the mind of the sender, as he thinks out the words to use, or it may be a mechanical device, such as the telephone or dictaphone. The more complicated the encoder, the greater the danger of communication failure.

The medium

The medium is the means by which the message is transmitted. It may be in written, spoken or visual format. The telephone line, a speech, an interview or a letter are all examples of a medium. The difficulty arises when the encoder is not properly adapted to the message: choosing a letter or memo where a meeting would have been more effective, for example.

The decoder

The decoder is basically the mind of the receiver. Decoding is an attempt to reconstruct the intended message from the message actually transmitted. Decoding takes place when the receiver frowns and says 'What does he mean?' If the code is not agreed or explained, the decoding will fail.

The receiver

The receiver is the person to whom the message is directed. The receiver has three duties: to listen to the message, decode it and transmit feedback to the sender.

Choosing the right media

Media can be classified into the following types (see Table 1).

Static media
Static media carry those types of communication that present the entire message to the receiver for decoding at one time. The sender is not present to alter the meaning or influence the reception of the message.

Dynamic media
These media carry constantly changing messages. The message is happening now and as such demands attention now. The message is in continual process.

Verbal media
The strengths and weaknesses of language are the strengths and weaknesses of verbal media. Words are only symbols that mean things to people. If they mean slightly different things to different people, they will cause imprecise communication. If the vocabulary of the receiver is smaller than that of the transmitter, some of the communication will be lost.

Non-verbal media
Non-verbal media avoid the use of human language: pictures, graphic images and gestures that do not rely on the spoken or written word to convey meaning. Non-verbal media can be very clear if the message is simple, but very confusing if the message is complicated.

Hot media
A hot medium provides a high degree of definition; that is, it is well filled with data. Hot media have been well thought out and planned and as such are usually not dynamic.

Cool media
Cool media contain less definition of data; they do not contain all the data necessary for precise communication. As a result, they require feedback and interaction.

Table 1. *Classification of media*

Media	Verbal	Non-verbal
Static	Books, magazines, reports, memoranda and other printed materials. Also notice boards, signposts, etc.	Photographs, paintings, cartoons, graphs and charts. Slides and filmstrips of non-verbal material.
Dynamic	The voice, tape recordings and radio. Soundtrack of films, TV and video tape.	Acting and gestures. Silent films. The visual content of TV. Puppet shows and pantomime.
Hot	Radio, books, letters, lectures and the soundtrack of films.	Photographs, slides and films.
Cool	Speech, telephone, TV, presentations and demonstrations.	Cartoons.

Obstacles to good communication

Obstacles to good communication come in two types: the obstacles placed by either the communicator or the person receiving the message, and the barriers erected by the recipient of the message. To avoid both the obstacles and the barriers, the two communicators need to experience empathy.

The following factors can be an obstacle to good communication:

- differences in perception;
- the context;
- external interference;
- internal interference.

Differences in perception
From the moment the sender begins to formulate his message, his personal motives, individual prejudices and psychology begin subtly to alter it. The manner in which the message is encoded partly reflects the way the sender sees the situation. No two individuals see the world in the same way; no two sets of assumptions and preconceived ideas are the same.

The context

Communication does not take place in a vacuum. Starting as mere words, the message gathers additional information and content along the way. The time, the place and the principals involved and their relation with each other will all add overtones to the message.

External interference

Loud noises, visual distractions, misaddressed letters and failed PA systems all disrupt communication because they distrupt concentration and distract one or both parties to the communication. Misplaced or unexplained jargon, confusing accents and wrong emphasis will all cause interference while the receiver tries to decode them.

Internal interference

Both the sender and the receiver may suffer from internal interference for the following reasons:

- *Assumptions:* Unexplained assumptions mean that the communication is out of context.
- *Preconceived ideas:* Preconceived ideas may lead the sender or the receiver to draw false conclusions.
- *Preoccupation:* The preoccupied sender or receiver cannot give the message his full attention. In such circumstances, it is likely that details are left out and the wrong message is transmitted. Too great a familiarity with the subject matter can often lead to the sender mistakenly taking certain knowledge for granted.
- *Anxiety:* The anxious receiver only hears the worst that he expected to hear. Anxiety blocks reception of the total message.
- *Distraction:* Certain trigger words may distract the receiver into word pictures of his own and result in lost attention to the message actually transmitted. Unless the receiver admits this and the message is repeated, totally false facts may be drawn from the transmission.

Overcoming barriers to communication

Apart from the obstacles put into the communication exercise by the sender, the receiver can cause communication breakdown with his own attitude.

The barriers to communication are the same of the causes of communication failure:

- not listening;
- dishonest feedback:
- poor feedback;
- judgements;
- stereotyping;
- emotions.

Not listening

People find it hard to listen. This is understandable, considering the fact that the human brain works at a rate of 600 words a minute, but the average human speaks at only 150 words per minute. Random thoughts fill the 450 word gap and the brain becomes distracted and loses full concentration. To listen actively:

- Sit up straight and breathe deeply to get maximum oxygen to the brain.
- Concentrate on the nouns and write them down.
- Watch for body language.
- Form mental questions relating to the message transmitted.
- Develop interest.

Dishonest feedback

Dishonest feedback is inaccurate feedback. People who do not understand and yet do not have the strength of character to say so may imply that they do understand and thereby prevent further explanation. Individuals in groups who nod and smile throughout a presentation are giving poor feedback; it is usually that they are not listening but rather giving signs that say 'Leave me alone, I agree with you.'

Poor feedback

Poor feedback is the lack of any feedback. If no feedback is forthcoming from dynamic or cool media, stop and ask for it.

Judgements

Judgements are a form of mental noise. Individuals tend to evaluate statements from their own point of view, without first considering the background of the sender. Each person's judgemental base is set in upbringing and early education, enhanced by personal experience and development, and as such is very difficult to set aside.

Stereotyping
It is very tempting to stereotype people that you meet. Background, age, religion, race, sex and dress are all generalisations that people tend to apply to the individual. Where the application of the generalisation is correct, no harm is done, but more often it is not correct and communication is broken. Think of the individual and get interested in him or her, and the barrier will fall away.

Emotions
Anger, frustration, anxiety and stress will all prevent the individual functioning to the full. Emotions cause people to rehearse conversations in their heads and then continue them in public without first introducing the receiver to the earlier part of the message. It may not be easy to control emotions, but it can be done.

- Think positive.
- Take nothing personally.
- Think of the sender not the message.
- Hear the true message not the emotions.

Empathy

The key to overcoming all the barriers to effective communication is empathy. Empathising with an individual is not easy but it can be done.

- Know yourself and your strengths and weaknesses.
- Learn to like yourself.
- Find a point of interest in the individual.
- Don't try to like people, it is a greater compliment to be interested.
- Understand what makes the other person tick.
- Don't try to change others.
- Try to learn from every situation.

Getting it right

Getting communication right means asking the following questions:

- *Who* - Who are you communicating with and what do they know?
- *What* - What do you have to communicate?
- *Where* - Where will the communication take place?
- *Why* - Why is this communication necessary?
- *When* - When should it take place?
- *How* - How and using what media can the message be best transmitted?

Supportive communication

Supportive communication is setting an unspoken atmosphere that is friendly, non-critical and non-threatening. Criticism is constructive; mistakes are for learning the right way. Most people fear change and as a result resist it; thus most communication is potentially threatening. Consequently, it is very likely to result in defensive anxious behaviour, instead of responsive behaviour.

Problem orientation
Don't try to persuade, try to relate to the problem. Let the receiver persuade himself while he talks it out.

Non-directive listening
Reduce return communication and therefore threatening behavioural patterns to a minimum. Listen, don't probe or react with your own views. Grunt, nod or restate what the speaker has just said. With your non-directive listening you may enable the speaker to talk out his problem. Most people seeking advice need this kind of help; they do not want a problem solved for them, they merely need the chance to talk about it and get it into proportion, thus solving it themselves.

Non-verbal communication

There is more to listening than using your ears. Non-verbal communication, body language, will signal your feelings to others all the time. You are probably already aware of this because of the problem caused by communicating on the telephone when you don't have the option of watching the body language message transmitted by the sender.

Use your body language to emphasise your message. The biggest mistakes are made when a body language message suggests disagreement, while the words used imply agreement. It is very important to ensure that body language matches the message being transmitted.

	You will seem defensive if you:
Face and head	Avoid eye contact or immediately look away when it occurs
	Don't look at the other person.
Hands and arms	Clench hands
	Cross arms
	Constantly rub an eye or nose or ear.
Body	Lean away from the other person
	Cross your legs
	Swivel your feet towards to door.
	You will seem anxious if you:
Face and head	Blink frequently
	Lick your lips
	Keep clearing your throat.
Hands and arms	Open and close your hands frequently
	Put your hand over your mouth while speaking
	Tug at an ear.
Body	Fidget in your chair
	Jig your feet up and down.
	You will seem aggressive if you:
Face and head	Stare at the other person
	Wear an 'I've heard it all before' smile
	Raise your eyebrows in exaggerated amazement or disbelief
	Look over the top of your spectacles.

Hands and arms	Point your finger at the other person Thump your fist on the table Rub the back of your neck.
Body	Stand while the other person remains seated Stride around Lean back in your chair with both hands behind your head and legs splayed.

You will seem friendly and co-operative if you:

Face and head	Look at the other person's face Smile Nod your head as the other person is talking.
Hands and arms	Have open hands Put your hand to your face occasionally Uncross your arms.
Body	Sit with uncrossed legs Lean slightly forward Move closer to the other person.

You will seem confident if you:

Face and head	Look into the other person's eyes Don't blink your eyes Thrust your chin forward.
Hands and arms	Keep your hands away from your face Steeple your fingers together Stand at ease with hands behind your back.
Body	When seated, you lean back with legs out in front of you Stand straight Stay still, make no sudden movements.

You will seem thoughtful if you:

Face and head	Look at the other person for three-quarters of the time when listening. Tilt your head to one side slightly.

Hands and arms	Stroke your chin or pinch the bridge of your nose Take off your spectacles and put the earpiece into your mouth.
Body	Lean forward to speak Lean back to listen Keep your legs still.

Transactional analysis

Transactional analysis is a system of understanding the mind which was first promoted by Dr Eric Berne. It considers the individual from the point of view of his behaviour and reactions.

Each individual is capable of responding to outside stimuli in three ways, and each of these is associated with an 'ego state'. The three ego states within each individual are:

- the parent ego state;
- the adult ego state;
- the child ego state.

Each ego state denotes a habitual way of thinking, feeling and behaving which occur together.

Ego states

Parent ego state
The parent is the part of an individual that reflects life as it is taught. It is the collection of all the things you do that your parents and other authority figures did, whether supporting or critical, including slogans, values and beliefs. The parent ego state:

- sets limits;
- disciplines;
- judges;
- criticises;
- gives advice and guidance;
- protects and nurtures;
- maintains traditions;
- makes rules and regulations about how life should be.

The parent subdivides into two different facets:

- *Critical parent* - sets limits and makes judgements about yourself and others.
- *Nurturing parent* - gives permission and support to yourself and others and allows you to grow and develop.

Adult ego state
The adult is the part of an individual that reflects life as it is thought and works things out by looking at the facts and making decisions as a result of what it sees. The adult state is unemotional and is concerned with what fits and what is most useful. The adult:

- gathers facts and data;
- sorts out the best alternatives;
- estimates probabilities;
- plans the steps in the decision-making process;
- questions.

Child ego state
The child is the part of an individual that reflects life as it is felt. It is the most important ego state in terms of control over your life. Personal change is not usually possible unless the energy in the child ego state is committed to the change. The child ego state is normally fixed by the time a person reaches six years of age. The child is the:

- centre of feelings;
- centre of energy;
- source of creativity, curiosity and intuition;
- site of your early experiences, including the way you have chosen to get attention from others.

The child ego state subdivides into two facets:

- *Free or natural child* - source of spontaneity, energy and curiosity. Often not visible in the grown human being until forced out with stimulants.
- *Adapted child* - Since to live with the free child is unacceptable in modern society, all individuals have produced the adapted child state. The adapted child shows the ways learned to get attention when small:
  — compliance;
  — procrastination;
  — rebellion.

There is a third function aspect of the child ego state which reflects the intuitive part that senses things about others in a flash - *Little Professor.*

Communication on the same wavelength

People who are speaking on the same wavelength are addressing like-minded individuals. When you make a joke and expect laughter, you are addressing the child ego state in another individual with your own child ego state. As long as the individual laughs at your joke, successful communication has been achieved.

Talking from the adult ego state to the equal ego state of the other person means using a cool, calm, collected attitude and not being aroused by emotions. It is far easier to communicate in business when you address one adult from your own adult viewpoint. This means that all the emotions must be removed and you must avoid upsetting any 'parental' viewpoint.

When the parent ego state is used it is essential to make sure that you address correctly the alter ego parent. You use your parental ego state when you sympathise with someone else about the inadequacies of a third party. That third party may well be your boss or your subordinate. The essence of the parent ego state is that the two parties agree on their apparent superiority and greater understanding.

Communication on the same wavelength should always be satisfactory because the two individuals understand each other.

Talking at cross purposes

When you speak at cross purposes it is because you use one ego state to address directly the ego state of your communicatee but they reply in an alternative ego state. You miss the point.

Parent to Parent: What a hopeless group of people!
Adult to Adult: It's not my problem, I have nothing to do with them.

Free Child to Nurturing Parent: I want advice.
Critical Parent to Adapted Child: Go and see someone else.

On being misunderstood

From time to time we address another adult from the adult ego state but do not receive an adult-to-adult reply. Very often the reply is either parent to child or child to parent. Since parent to child and child to parent are satisfactory communications, although less effective in business, it is very easy for them to continue and to transfer the communication into parent to child/child to parent. The end effect is to give the wrong impression and to cause irritation.

Adult to adult: I've taken it as far as I can go and I've hit a problem.
Parent to Child: Oh give it to me, you're hopeless.
Child to Parent: Fine, I won't bother to try any more.

On misleading

From time to time you speak from the adult state to the adult ego state of another individual. However, sometimes your body language does not match the ego state you are using. Indeed, very often the body language implies a hidden message either by actual phrases, or tone, or maybe just gestures. This is a style of communication that can be deliberately used to mislead; it is a favourite technique of salesmen. They point out to you, using their adult ego state, all the advantages of the product they are advising you to purchase, but give the hidden message that you should be purchasing a larger or more expensive product because it would better match your own view of life. Many of us instinctively respond to the ego message they have offered us and choose to buy the larger or more expensive product. An example of such deliberate misleading is as follows:

Adult to Adult: I am sure you are quite correct in assuming that the cheaper model is more practical for you. However, we often find that people in your status in life choose the larger model.
Parent to Child: The hidden message is simply that if you wish to enhance your status in life you will buy the more expensive model.
Child to Parent: My personal ego state requires that I purchase the larger one thus speaking out loud, 'Yes, I will choose the more expensive item.'

Controlling information into the system

If you do not tell people what they want to know, they will find out a half-truth by using the grapevine. A grapevine exists in every organisation; sometimes its activities are amusing, often they are not. The active grapevine is the one operating in an organisation where the management feels that staff do not need to know, or where they simply do not think about telling staff the facts. There are some basic truths about the grapevine:

- Grapevines never publish good news.
- People believe the grapevine rather than the management.
- Grapevines spread demotivation and dissatisfaction.
- Grapevines exaggerate and distort.
- You lose the best people as a result of grapevine rumour.
- Clients and customers get to hear the rumours too.
- The staff you'd like to lose stay and spread the grapevine further.

To stay alive in communication, minimise the work of the grapevine. You can never get rid of it entirely, but you can cut it down to size. Information kills grapevines.

How to inform
- Hold a meeting:
  - full staff;
  - sections;
  - one to one.
- Write:
  - detailed memos;
  - reports;
  - personal letters;
  - office manuals;
  - posters.
- Publish:
  - on a notice board;
  - in-house magazine.

Meetings
To be effective, a meeting must be the right size for the information to be communicated.

- If it affects everybody, tell them all at once.
- If it affects departments in different ways, tell them department by department.
- If it really affects only one person, tell them one to one.
- If it affects one person most, tell that person and then hold a full meeting to inform others.
- In doubt? Tell too many people rather than too few.

Written word
The written word must match its audience and elucidate rather than confuse, as follows:

- Memos for detailed information.
- Reports to express opinions.
- Letters to deal with personal or private matters.
- Office manuals for detailed information that needs to be kept.
- Posters to emphasise salient points.

Publish
Some information is of a general nature that needs to be seen by self-selected staff; publication is the best method of sending it out. Do not rely on this method for information that *must* be read and assimilated by all.

- Put up notices on the notice board about social matters and general interest matters.
- Use the notice board to display auxiliary posters to back-up other more detailed information.
- Print articles and news in the in-house magazine.

Notice board. There are certain rules that need to be applied to the notice board:

- Correct siting means it will be read:
  — a well-lit spot where loiterers do not block movement;
  — somewhere where people have time to stop and read it.
- Incorrect siting means it will be ignored:
  — a dark corner in the middle of a busy corridor;
  — somewhere no one normally goes.
- Untidy notice boards say no one cares:
  — don't leave out-of-date notices up;
  — small boards look neater;
  — collect relevant information together;
  — make someone responsible for the board.
- Use the most easily read parts of the board for the most important notices:
  — eye-level left-hand side;
  — eye-level centre and right-hand side;
  — upper parts of the board.

In-house magazines: It is not only the largest organisations that benefit from the publication of in-house magazines. Nor does the magazine have to be glossy and expensive. The key criteria for a good in-house magazine are:

- interest;
- relevance;
- visual;
- publication at expected time.

Communication mix
Getting the right message across usually means using the right communication mix to emphasise at the right moment.

Announcing a new product or service
- Give details in a full staff meeting.
- Confirm the announcement with a bulletin on the notice board.
- Publish full details in the house magazine.
- Tell the world with PR and advertising.

Informing employees of detailed changes to the operating system
- Send memos giving outline details and warning of impending changes.
- Send detailed sheets for the office procedures manual.
- Call section meetings to explain and train.
- Use posters in the following weeks to remind staff.

Remember
Finally, to control information into the system:

- Keep it simple.
- Make it direct.
- Show rather than tell.
- Say too much not too little.
- Warn in advance.
- Remember you are talking to individuals.

Further Reading from Kogan Page

Don't Do, Delegate! The Secret Power of Successful Managers,
   James M Jenks and John M Kelly
The Effective Communicator, John Adair
Effective Interviewing, John Fletcher
Effective Performance Appraisals, Robert B Maddux
The Effective Supervisor, John Adair
Essential Management Checklists, Jeffrey P Davidson
The Fifty-Minute Supevisor: A Guide for the Newly Promoted,
   Elwood N Chapman
The First-Time Manager, M J Morris
A Handbook of Management Techniques, Michael Armstrong
How To Be An Even Better Manager, Michael Armstrong
How To Develop Your Personal Management Skills, Jane Allan
How To Make Meetings Work, Malcolm Peel
Managing Disagreement Constructively, Herbert S Kindler
Readymade Interview Questions, Malcolm Peel
Winning Strategies for Managing People; A Task-Directed Guide,
   Robert Irwin and Rita Wolenik